NEW DIRECTIONS
FOR COLLEGE
LEARNING ASSISTANCE

Number 2 • 1980

NEW DIRECTIONS FOR COLLEGE LEARNING ASSISTANCE

A Quarterly Sourcebook
Kurt V. Lauridsen, Editor-in-Chief

Number 2, 1980

New Roles for Learning Assistance

Oscar T. Lenning
Robbie L. Nayman
Guest Editors

Jossey-Bass Inc., Publishers
San Francisco • Washington • London

NEW ROLES FOR LEARNING ASSISTANCE
New Directions for College Learning Assistance
Number 2, 1980
    Oscar T. Lenning, Robbie L. Nayman, Guest Editors

New Directions for College Learning Assistance is published quarterly
by Jossey-Bass Inc., Publishers. Subscriptions are available
at the regular rate for institutions, libraries, and agencies
of $30 for one year. Individuals may subscribe at the special
professional rate of $18 for one year.

Correspondence:
Subscriptions, single-issue orders, change of address notices,
undelivered copies, and other correspondence should be sent to
New Directions Subscriptions, Jossey-Bass Inc., Publishers,
433 California Street, San Francisco, California 94104.

Editorial correspondence should be sent to the Editor-in-Chief,
Kurt V. Lauridsen, Director, Student Learning Center,
University of California, Berkeley, California 94720.

Library of Congress Catalogue Card Number LC 79-92041
International Standard Serial Number ISSN 0271-0617
International Standard Book Number ISBN 87589-805-X

Cover design by Willi Baum
Manufactured in the United States of America

Contents

Editors' Notes Oscar T. Lenning **vii**
Robbie L. Nayman

The Learning Center: Toward an Gwyn Enright **1**
Expanded Role Gene Kerstiens

The authors present an overview of the development of learning centers
in higher education and their current evolution.

Learning Centers and the Faculty: James W. Shaw **25**
Improving Academic Competency

A faculty member and administrator at a major institution outlines how
learning centers and faculty members can achieve a mutually beneficial
working relationship.

Learning Centers and Instructional/ June Dempsey **41**
Curricular Reform Barbara Tomlinson

The authors describe functional strategies that learning specialists can
use to stimulate and implement reforms in traditional college curriculums and instruction.

Learning Centers and Retention Philip E. Beal **59**

The role that learning centers can play in assisting institutionwide retention efforts is outlined. Various strategies currently used in improving
student persistence fall within the area of learning assistance services.

Evaluating Learning Centers Robert R. Brown **75**

Guidelines for conducting evaluation of services offered in learning centers are provided.

The Past, Present, and Future for Oscar T. Lenning **93**
Learning Centers Robbie L. Nayman

The volume is summarized and possibilities of new and expanded services that may become part of learning center operations in the future
are considered.

Index **101**

Editors' Notes

The common theme running through all of the chapters of this volume is that the concept of a learning center needs to be expanded, as regards both its purpose and scope. Another common theme is that, for such expansion to occur, a more holistic, campus-wide orientation that adapts effectively to political realities and other factors must become operative.

In the first chapter, Gwyn Enright and Gene Kerstiens help us to view learning centers from a historical perspective. They describe the origin of learning centers, their emergence as a student service, the rationale for their existence, possible prototype centers that currently exist on one or more college campuses, current issues of concern, and trends for the future. The current issues of concern include the relation of assistance to resources, the appropriate target population, how the learning-disabled student should be regarded and treated, the factors related to mastery learning, whether credit should be awarded, the affective versus the cognitive approach, staffing arrangements, status and stature, staff development leadership, the role of instructional innovation and implementation, and the institutionalization of learning centers.

In the next chapters, James Shaw and then June Dempsey and Barbara Tomlinson focus, in process terms, on how to expand the role of learning centers in the areas of academic competencies and instructional and curricular improvement. The importance of getting faculty involved, and how best to go about doing that, is discussed in some depth. Such areas as individualization, flexibility of approach, and accountability are also introduced.

Next, Philip Beal reports on a national survey of action programs that have been implemented to improve student retention. He then focuses on how learning centers succeeded as action programs for increasing student retention, and he suggests that a number of other successful action programs could conceivably be activities of learning centers.

Robert Brown then emphasizes the importance of evaluating learning centers and their impact, defines evaluation, and demonstrates how to make effective and efficient evaluations. The learning center director who studies Brown's model and practical guidelines for conducting evaluations of learning centers will see that such evaluations can be realistic, feasible, and effective.

Finally, Oscar Lenning and Robbie Nayman provide an overview and integration of the preceding chapters and present some thoughts for the future.

Oscar T. Lenning
Robbie L. Nayman
Guest Editors

Oscar T. Lenning, senior associate at the National Center for Higher Education Management Systems (NCHEMS), joined the NCHEMS staff in 1974 after eight years on the research staff of the American College Testing Program. He has also served as a college counselor, student activities director, memorial union night manager, and secondary school teacher. His research and publications have dealt primarily with students, college outcomes and goals, prediction, evaluation, needs assessment, data collection and application, planning, and communication.

Robbie L. Nayman, senior psychologist, University Counseling Center and assistant professor, Department of Education, Colorado State University, is past chairperson of Commission XVI—Learning Centers in Higher Education—of the American College Personnel Association (ACPA). Her publications and research interests are in the areas of the professionalization of learning centers, student development services for adult students, and program development and evaluation for multiethnic minorities.

In responding to the diverse and changing needs of an
ever-challenging population of learners, learning centers
have expanded their functions, accelerated their
influence, generated and catalyzed academic issues,
and promoted attitudes, methodologies, and strategies
that promise to alter and improve higher education.

The Learning Center:
Toward an Expanded Role

Gwyn Enright
Gene Kerstiens

History

The learning center first appeared in the professional literature about 1970 (Carman, 1970; Christ, 1971; Ellison, 1970; Gunselman, 1971). For the next ten years, educational journals, monographs, anthologies, and guides were replete with articles and chapters in which writers marveled at and reveled in the multiplicity of names for learning centers. At least fifteen different titles have been counted (Enright, 1975, p. 88), but one report recorded that eighteen of the thirty-eight two-year college centers surveyed used the word *learning* in their title (McPherson and others, 1976, p. 5). Of course, the variety of titles mirrors the diversity of learning center missions, services, audiences, locations, and affiliations.

The terminological inconsistency has made it possible for the learning center to assume different meanings. It has been described as an *answer* to the needs and demands of new students (Clymer, 1978; Park, 1976; Sullivan, 1978), as an *activity* to provide materials and expertise for university instructors (Merrill and Drob, 1977), as a *merger* of reading and study skills programs with tutorial services (Maxwell, 1979), and as a *marriage* of instruction and technology (Kerstiens, 1971). It has also been described as a *place* for nontraditional learning (Peterson, 1975), for instruction not usually included in the college classroom (McPherson and others, 1976), or for course-related support, where one might find the "combined atmospheres of a medical clinic, a mechanics shop, and a coffee house" (Roueche and Snow, 1977, p. 124). This terminology reflects the evolution of the learning center and the snowball sequence of its development (Enright, 1975). Published descriptions and reports can be used to trace the history of the learning center from its origins in study skills classes, counseling services for World War II veterans, and nonprint library collections to the present concept of a campus-wide academic support service.

1850–1940. As early as the mid nineteenth century, college and university administrators and instructors were troubled by the problems presented by poor students. In his 1852 inaugural address, University of Michigan president Henry P. Tappan warned that universities were lowering their standards by admitting poorly prepared students (Maxwell, 1979). In spite of such helping measures as orientation, freshman conference (Andrews, 1932), and college preparatory programs — implemented as early as 1862 and operational in 350 colleges by 1915 (Maxwell, 1979, p. 7) — the problems persisted. In 1907, more than half of the enrolled students at Harvard, Yale, Princeton, and Columbia universities failed to meet the entrance requirements (Maxwell, 1979, p. 8), and in 1926 one half of the University of Indiana freshmen failed to satisfy their course requirements, with 16 percent of the students flunking at least half of their classes in the first semester (Book, 1927, p. 529). Yet by 1930, at least in California, the public was reasonably comfortable with the idea that all students should be allowed to pursue postsecondary education (Morgan, 1930).

The idea that underprepared students, and even well-equipped students, could learn to become better students or "learn to learn" also dates from the early twentieth century. Study techniques guides written for college students (Robinson, 1941; Von KleinSmid and Touton, 1929; Whipple, 1916) supported the sentiment that potentially good students could be salvaged if they knew how to study (Behrens, 1935; Book, 1927; Sharp, 1943) or knew the "tricks of the scholar's trade" (Andrews, 1932, p. 388).

Programs in which study skills training was provided were typically short-term (Eckert and Jones, 1935) and addressed to freshmen or probationary students (Behrens, 1935; Book, 1927); they emphasized study management (Eckert and Jones, 1935) as well as reading, writing, and math skills (Garland, 1978b; Maxwell, 1979). The positive outcomes of these enterprises underscored both the importance of scheduling skills instruction during the regular semester or quarter and the advantage of offering redemptive education on an elective basis.

Precursors of modern learning assistance modes, early college preparatory programs were revised into how-to-study courses attended by both freshmen and upperclassmen in academic distress. Taught during the regular semester by English, psychology, or education faculty, these classes treated reading, time management, study environment (McGann, 1948), outlining, notetaking, preparing for and taking exams, library skills (Eckert and Jones, 1935), and memory and concentration (McGann, 1948), and they included applications to actual class assignments (Book, 1927; Sharp, 1943) and attention to psychological as well as physical health care (Behrens, 1935). Of the institutions offering remedial programs, four out of nine awarded college credit for compensatory work (Parr, 1930, p. 548). Nevertheless, although the classes produced student gains as evidenced by grades, pre/posttests, persistence, survey results, and "efficiency ratios," they did not significantly influence students' relative class ranking (Andrews, 1932; Eckert and Jones, 1935).

During this era, student support programs looked for answers in clinical, analytical, and scientific sources. One exemplary remedial reading program conducted by Luella C. Pressey at Ohio State University included instruction in eye movements and vocal processes and "phrase reading by means of a tachistoscope which threw the phrases upon a screen" (Parr, 1930, p. 548). This instrumentation from the psychology laboratory (Spache, 1969) was embraced wholeheartedly by reading teachers. Of the skills addressed in the how-to-study classes, reading improvement was identified as the most scientific approach to saving students and, therefore, the most promising. Accordingly, reading itself began to be taught, not as a part of another course but as a course or program in itself. In 1936, New York University initiated the first reading laboratory (Maxwell, 1979).

1940–1950. Remedial reading programs raised high hopes in the early nineteen forties (Wittenborn, 1944; Witty, 1940). Surveys revealed that between 30 percent and 60 percent of the colleges and universities polled either had operational programs or planned to offer programs by 1942 (Charters, 1941; Triggs, 1942; Witty, 1940; Zerga, 1940). As a general rule, credit was not awarded for these courses (Bear, 1950; Witty, 1940), except in the junior colleges (Zerga, 1940).

Remedial reading was not considered part of regular class instruction (Charters, 1941). Occasionally, reading classes were augmented by supplementary practice outside of class (Wittenborn, 1944) or by personal conferences (Robinson, 1945; Triggs, 1942). Instrumentation was still considered the mark of the modern program, though only three of twenty-two institutions surveyed used such equipment as the Keystone Opthalmic Telebinocular, Ophthalm-O-Graph, and Metronoscope in 1940 (Zerga, 1940, p. 195). However, in 1946 eleven of twenty-six institutions reported using such instrumentation (Walker,

1946, p. 120). For diagnosing reading handicaps and for offering an informal, personal atmosphere, the laboratory was deemed more appropriate than the classroom (Charters, 1941; Robinson, 1945). Emphasis was placed on laboratory practice for the "acquisition of good study habits rather than on theoretical discussions of the best study methods" (Sharp, 1943, p. 271) because "theory was merely a thread which makes practice intelligent" (Charters, 1941, p. 119).

In addition to providing for independent practice, feasible individualization, and clinical diagnosis (Triggs, 1942), the laboratory also housed such equipment as film projectors and "recording machines" (Walker, 1946, p. 120). In 1942, one reading program used a methodology similar to one used in many learning centers today. Triggs described a six-week program at the University of Minnesota where students engaged in activities prescribed in conference with an instructor and written into folders in order to remedy their most serious weaknesses, which had been identified by administration of a diagnostic test battery. Although the instructor was available for conferences, a lab assistant monitored students' progress (Triggs, 1942).

This move toward individualization necessitated new materials. Although it was conceded that commercial materials were more motivating for students, many instructors developed their own lab materials (Charters, 1941; Simpson, 1942). Many of these early instructional development products were modular and self-instructional. In fact, the need for new materials was great enough to warrant a marketing research study by the University of Minnesota Press (Triggs, 1942).

In addition to materials development, reading instructors were already engaged in efforts to change their colleague's viewpoint as well as their teaching. Their persistent attempts to persuade subject matter or content-area instructors to include reading instruction in their courses (Bear, 1950; McGann, 1948) could be considered early faculty development enterprises. "For the long run, one of the best contributions of the reading service could be the education of faculty members regarding their opportunities and responsibilities for the reading growth of their students" (Bear, 1950, p. 579).

Reading programs continued to be administered by English, education, and psychology departments and by guidance programs. Occasionally, departments shared administrative responsibility (Bond, 1940). Often, the library was a partner in the reading program (Bear, 1950; Bond, 1940). For example, the University of Florida library offered its students "self-administering" reading tests (Bear, 1950). According to a 1947–48 survey of 165 college and university reading programs, 25 percent were administered by English departments, 21 percent by education departments, 19 percent by counseling and testing programs, 14 percent by psychology departments, and 18 percent by two or more areas (Bear, 1950, p. 577).

In the aftermath of World War II the expansion of academic support services accelerated. This affected the development of the learning center in several ways. Many support services, such as counseling and condensed short-term remedial classes originally initiated through the G.I. Bill for former servicemen, later became available to all students (Maxwell, 1979). In addition, technology developed during the war, such as operations control systems, would later be applied to education and to the learning center (Saettler, 1978). Weiner's *Cybernetics,* published in 1948, was destined to be the foundation for the systems approach used in later learning centers (Saettler, 1978).

By 1950, the term *remedial* had fallen from grace. The label was to be avoided (Bear, 1950; Delong, 1948; Wittenborn, 1944), since reading instruction was considered relevant to *all* students, not just to "the victims of a system that produces casualties" (Witty, 1940, p. 568). The finer distinctions "remedial/developmental" (Walker, 1946, p. 121) and "handicapped/corrective/developmental" (Bear, 1950, p. 575) were suggested as more accurate and palatable. Several authors proposed that remedial instruction should not only serve a wider range of students but also that it should not be confined to a single emphasis (Delong, 1948; Simpson, 1942); as one of them put it, there are "various means of getting from the beginning to the end of a college course" (Delong, 1948, p. 121). In his address at the Annual Institute on Reading at Temple University, Bear (1950) shared his conviction that one should avoid setting up a program which promotes a single technique or skill, since this practice is based upon the notions that all students learn the same way and that there is one best approach for all students. These are oversimplifications.

Signifying as they do the movement toward considering multiple answers to complex questions, toward searching out the right solution for each student, the attempts to provide instructional alternatives in the counseling, English, or education areas were not compatible with developments in what was becoming known as audiovisual education, where practitioners were intrigued by multiple strategies and mixed-media methods (Kemp and others, 1980). Just as the psychology laboratory contributed diagnostic tools and a scientific approach to reading instruction, psychology would influence the heavily device-oriented audiovisual field, where instructional technology meant mechanical technology and where individual differences had yet to be recognized (Saettler, 1978).

1950–1960. The prediction that within the next decade the terms *remedial* and *developmental* would give way to *communication arts* (Walker, 1946, p. 121) portends the popularity attained in the nineteen fifties by "fusion courses," which combined reading, writing, listening, and speaking skills. While communications skills courses were criticized as too general and as premature for students lacking basic skills

(Angus, 1958), they integrated skills that were considered aspects of a single process (Blake, 1955; Gregory, 1958) and embodied the trend toward looking at the whole person. Attention was directed to the study skills, personality variables, and intellectual factors involved in reading and writing (Bamman, 1954; Tresselt and Richlin, 1951; Weber, 1954), and exemplary courses addressed both academic achievement and personality adjustment (Tresselt and Richlin, 1951). Personality problems, considered the most important factor in study skills gains (Tresselt and Richlin, 1951), were treated in the interview part of such programs, which combined lecture, group session, and interview modes (Tresselt and Richlin, 1951); small-group, individual study, and counseling sessions (Spache and others, 1959); or lecture, laboratory, and tutoring components (Blake, 1956). To administer these multifaceted programs, Blake recommended that a multidisciplinary committee govern a nondepartmental unit (1955), and Gregory pointed out the attractive team-teaching alternative that was available when communication skills were not relagated to a single department (1958).

The growth of developmental programs that were "tailored to the specific needs of the students" (Spache and others, 1959) and that also recognized the "total learning experience of the student" (Gregory, 1958, p. 205) was aided by the introduction of programmed materials. By the late 1950s, B. F. Skinner's ideas were being incorporated into programmed learning materials (Maxwell, 1979, p. 108). In 1959, the University of Florida College Reading Program served 700 largely self-referred students, offering each student a diagnostic workup, a posttest counseling session, a detailed written prescription of activities, and materials organized to the nth degree that were available to students on a drop-in basis in the lab (Spache and others, 1959). According to Spache, who described one approach to programmed materials, the materials "represent a gradual evolution of appropriate exercises and instructional materials in each reading habit or selections from a multitude of sources. We would take a chapter from a how-to-study manual on the problem of concentration, let us say, write an introduction, and a number of questions helping him to understand and clarify his insight and try this out with a number of students until we had decided whether it seems to be helpful. In this fashion, materials have been gradually revised and rewritten" (1959, p. 38).

Programmed materials were based on specified learner objectives, and the management by objectives orientation of the learning center today had origins in the acceptance and utilization of learner goals and program objectives in the late nineteen fifties. MacDonald, describing the Marquette University reading and study skills programs, emphasized that students were never competing against a norm in the lab, but concerned only with meeting their own goals for learner improvement (Deterline, 1968; Spache and others, 1959). Just as objectives were stated in order to measure student progress, goals were also set for programs to enable them to be evaluated (Blake, 1956; Durkee, 1952; Gregory, 1958). Blake (1955, 1956), for instance, points to the need for research to indicate the improvements that ought to be undertaken and also to show whether "set goals" had been met.

1960-1970. In the nineteen sixties, political necessity, learning theory, and technological reality came together to spur the development of the first learning centers. The sentiment expressed by Durkee (1952, p. 30)—"Once the college admits a student, it assumes a moral and educational obligation to do all that it can to provide for his development"—would have a heavy ring by the end of the decade. Many of the colleges and universities that opened their doors to the poor and the underprepared in order to give equal access to higher education and the social and economic advantages promised by education (Cross, 1971; Knoell, 1970) had no hint of the complications to follow. "For such colleges, this venture into mass education usually began abruptly, amidst the misgivings of administrators, who had to guess in the dark about the sorts of programs they ought to plan for students they had never met, and the reluctancies of teachers, some of whom had already decided that the new students were ineducable" (Shaughnessy, 1977, p. 1). By 1970, one in every seven students enrolled in colleges and universities in the United States would come from poverty backgrounds (Maxwell, 1979, p. 11), and the enrollment problem would be redefined not as one of recruitment but as one of retention (Knoell, 1970).

Desperation may have accelerated the acceptance of educational innovations in the nineteen sixties. At any rate, programmed instruction, influenced by Skinner and Crowder, was adapted and used in college reading programs as early as 1962 (Raygor and Summers, 1963), in spite of fears that it would render instruction "teacher-proof" (Meierhenry, 1980). The materials used in programmed instruction not only allowed for individualization but were also the catalyst for a substantial reorganization of instruction. The peer tutoring programs pioneered in California community colleges between 1969 and 1972 to serve the new students (Woolley, 1976, p. 41) played a similar role. In the reading laboratory, tutors were trained as technicians and as facilitators; their influence, together with continuing technological advances, helped to alter traditional patterns of instruction. Instructors began to see themselves as guides, not as performers (Newman, 1966). Bloom's notion of mastery learning, which allowed students to learn at their own pace until they reached a predetermined level of proficiency, became the basis of developmental education programs and learning centers (Roueche and Pitman, 1972). The orientation of the field that by 1970 would be termed *educational communications and technology* shifted from thing toward learners, and communication theory was woven with technological advances into a system dedicated to real improvements in learning and instruction. Instructional television, which had been well received by students if not by faculty, was explored (Donisi, 1962; Neidt, 1967; "TV Retention and Learning," 1958) and both computer-assisted instruction (Suppes and Macken, 1978; Suppes and Morningstar, 1969; Watson and Luskin, 1972; Williams, 1967) and computer-managed instruction (Kersteins, 1970; Williams, 1967) were used. "Systems" joined the argot of learning center literature, with the San Bernardino Valley College Learning Center being probably the first center to use a systems approach (Williams, 1967), while the *SR/SE Laboratory* was probably the first study skills curriculum based on systems (Christ, 1969).

By 1970, learning centers had replaced reading laboratories and study skills programs. Associated with counseling programs, the library, or English or psychology departments, the early centers had little uniformity in function and no preconceived sense of purpose on campus. Often, the center was an accommodative device. Adult education offerings in the learning laboratory could easily be expanded to include college learning skills (Brown, 1965), and the library-affiliated learning center was appropriate for centralization and innovation (Balanoff, 1963; Jones, 1966). Some learning centers inherited their goals from librarians who showed little enthusiasm for nonprint media (Fusario, 1970) or from counselors averse to specializing in study skills counseling (Kirk, 1969). By the end of the decade, however, there were indications that programs and practitioners had broadened their concepts. Perhaps the first center designed to offer academic support services to all students and to operate not as a reading center but as a learning center that cut across curricular boundaries (G. Williams, 1971) was the Study Skills Center at Lane Community College (Ellison, 1970).

The rapid growth of the learning center movement was due in part to the dismal failure of remedial and compensatory programs based on special classes (Kendrick and Thomas, 1970; Maxwell, 1979; Roueche, 1968). It seems likely that many of these remedial programs were token efforts—initiated hurriedly, somewhat desparately, with modest commitment, and only to enable institutions to point to an agency that lent credibility to an open enrollment policy that was voiced though barely tolerated by faculty and administration (Kersteins, 1971). By the end of the nineteen sixties, dissatisfaction with institutional efforts aimed at salvaging students essentially by having them major in remediation (Maxwell, 1979)—80 percent of these students chose not to enroll in college credit classes (Roueche and Snow, 1977)—led to hopes for approaches that did not isolate students from the regular curriculum, that attended to student affect, and that also worked to achieve more efficient and effective learning in the college classroom and lecture hall.

1970–1980. In the nineteen seventies, learning centers flourished, and professional interest focused on counting, categorizing, conceptualizing, and evaluating learning centers. A 1974 survey that yielded 1,258 responses revealed that of 761 institutions having reading/study skills programs or learning centers, 57 percent became operational after 1970 (Devirian, Enright, and Smith, 1975). In addition, 115 institutions had plans to initiate learning centers by 1976. While community colleges boasted a greater number of such programs and centers in 1974 (Smith, Enright, and Devirian, 1975), four-year institutions were leading the way by 1979 (Sullivan, 1978). In 1978, a comprehensive survey identified 1,848 learning centers on 1,433 campuses in the United States and Canada (Sullivan, 1978).

In 1971, Frank Christ formulated the concept of the learning assistance center as a "place concerned with the learning environment within and without, functioning primarily to enable students to learn more in less time with greater ease and confidence; offering tutorial help, study aids in the content areas, and referrals to other helping agencies; and serving as a testing ground for innovative machines, materials, and programs" (Christ, 1971, p. 35). Effectively integrating instruction, technology, and counseling within a systems fabric that was syncrgistic, cybernetic, and mathemagenic (Spann, 1979), the learning assistance center offered academic support to all learners on the college or university campus (Spann, 1979). Because the learning assistance center promoted an intelligent and humane use of technology in a multidisciplinary, nondepartmental context, it was frequently replicated, and it has become one of the most clearly identifiable examples of the generic term *learning center.*

Attempts to define and delimit the learning center (Carman, 1970; Merren, 1975; McPherson and others, 1976; Peterson, 1973, 1975; Touhey, 1970) resulted in such terms as *learning skills center* (McPherson and others, 1976), which refers to a departmental center offering reading, writing, or mathematics instruction, often on a drop-in basis; *learning resource center* and *learning center* (Ellison, 1973; Peterson, 1973; See, 1974), which refer to a comprehensive facility that includes instructional development in addition to learning development services (Sullivan, 1978); and *learning assistance center* (Bock, 1978). One widely accepted model (Peterson, 1975) has four components: nontraditional learning spaces, instructional development, a library, and audiovisual services.

In the past decade, learning center theorists and practitioners have directed their attention to promising avenues for helping students remain in school and succeed. Addressing affect and personality, they have used applications of motivation theory (Roueche and Mink, 1976), behavior modification, and cognitive-style mapping. Viewing scheduling and course outlines from the student's perspective, they developed minicourses (Brown and others, 1977; Johnson and Peterson, 1972) and adjunct courses (Bergman, 1977; Carpenter and Jones, 1976; Enright, 1979; Mayfield, 1977; Tomlinson and Tomlinson, 1976), which serve to connect skills development to content-area classes more clearly (Kazmierski, 1971).

Learning centers make use of media and machines, which cause people to see them as an "impersonal outgrowth of mass production" (Maxwell, 1979, p. 104). Thus an ombudsman function to put the centers firmly on the side of the students was needed (Garland, 1978a; Kerstiens, 1972a). "In college, one must adapt to the rituals and requirements in order to succeed, sometimes compromising one's own interests and needs with the demands and constraints set by faculty members and administrators. Learning centers exist to help students make this adjustment" (Maxwell, 1979, p. 104). Withholding judgment on the educational goals of the faculty and the students (Henderson, Melloni, and Sherman, 1971), the learning center professional embraced the philosophy of change agent (Hultgren, 1970; Kerstiens, 1972a; Swindling, 1977), upheld technology as a way of thinking (Fraley and Vargas, 1975), and assumed the role of watchdog (Enright, 1975), hoping to be more than just an appendage to an outdated, if not corrupt, educational industry (Cross, 1976; Saettler, 1978).

Current Issues

Understandably, the use of learning centers in higher education has generated controversy. Because learning centers have grown rapidly in number, served a largely nontraditional student population, invaded disciplinary boundaries, and because they are eclectically innovative, their propriety has often been questioned by the academic establishment. Within the movement itself, opinions differ on the legitimacy or feasibility of certain concepts, designs, approaches, and strategies that have been employed by learning centers. Consequently, an unapologetic exploration of the debate on some issues that has been inspired or catalyzed by the learning center movement will allow us to explain the nature and direction of its expanding role.

Assistance Versus Resources. When learning center staff and directors search for an academic mission, they have one of two options for the emphasis or comprehensiveness of the services that they will provide. One option (pro-learning assistance) is based on the following rationale: Since the curriculum and the typical lecture-classroom-textbook presentation that prevails in higher education today will continue into the indefinite future, and since increasing numbers of students need basic and/or academic skills in order to be successful with this curriculum, these students should be helped to obtain the necessary skills for classroom learning. The other option (pro-learning resources) may be stated thusly: Since a growing number of students possess talent for learning and achieving, although not in the traditional sense, and since these students can learn effectively through new modes of delivery, it is necessary to use advances in instructional media and technology to redesign and/or enrich conventional offerings. One option emphasizes the need for learning skills and prepares the student to accommodate himself to the instructional status quo, while the other views curriculum and instruction as in need of reform and sets out to change learning conditions to accommodate learners (Clark, 1980; Cross, 1979).

While any learning center could offer programs and services that reflect only one of these positions, we do not wish to suggest that this would be ideal or that it was the result of philosophical persuasion or prejudice, although there is some evidence that dissension exists (McClung, 1977). Indeed, the two approaches are hardly incompatible, and a comprehensive learning center will offer services that attempt to fulfill both expectations. Rather, the emphasis exerted by a given center more often reflects the expertise or enthusiasm of the center director and staff, the intramural environment for instructional change, the political temperament, and the architectural flexibility of the campus itself. Indeed, the significant question is not whether to renovate instruction or to remediate students, but where and when to employ limited energies and budget to best improve the learning environment.

Target Population. While most learning center directors and practitioners view their services as being designed to assist the entire campus community (Guskin and Greenbaum, 1979), there are those who see its function as chiefly remedial, in the most pejorative sense (Cross, 1976). Therefore certain student ability groups can become the target for de facto inclusion or exclusion. Some administrations and faculties have established such goals that the learning center at their institution can be seen as a protective device separating traditional faculty from inept students by keeping low achievers in a holding pattern until they reach an acceptable level of academic behavior (Guskin and Greenbaum, 1979; McPherson and others, 1976). However, other learning centers have been found to be effective and popular even at academically prestigious colleges and universities ("Help for the Brightest," 1976; Roueche and Snow, 1977; Walker and others, 1974), and most centers view their clientele as naturally and interestingly heterogenous.

The Learning-Disabled Student. Another problem involving the population to be served is the question of whether learning-disabled students should be diagnosed and given assistance. The fact that students with learning disorders have chosen to pursue higher education is hardly news (McAllister and others, 1972). Incalculable numbers of these students have lived up to their own expectations of failure, which are shared by the institutions. However, the political climate is changing, and strict interpretation of Section 504 of the Rehabilitation Act of 1973 mandates appropriate auxiliary services for such students. They are now guaranteed accessibility to higher education (Lombardi, 1979b). Moreover, recent court decisions indicate that institutions unresponsive to the needs of the learning-disabled may be charged with malpractice ("A Question of Malpractice," 1978) and give legal authority to the principle that all students have an "acknowledged right to proper diagnosis, accurate classification, accurate information regarding performance, and appropriate instruction" (McCarthy, 1979, p. 211).

To further complicate the issue, the term *learning disabilities* has been interpreted in many ways (Reger, 1979). This can cause honest confusion, and it can also be turned to the advantage of someone who wants to avoid responsibility. However, Sullivan's (1975) definition seems to place the term in reasonable perspective:

> Operationally, the concept of learning disabilities includes those educational factors within a student's learning style that impair rapid learning practices. This approach implies that such factors are not related to mental retardation, emotional disturbance, physical handicaps, visual or aural impairment, and that appropriate curricular and instructional responses can assist the learner in overcoming the disability [p. 6].

This definition is applicable to the growing college population that can be "certified" as developmentally learning disabled as well as the even greater number of students who are classified as "new learners." It also mitigates charges that severely disabled students would be given custodial care rather than meaningful instructional therapy (Lombardi, 1979b). For these reasons, and also because enabling legislation has funded programs for learning-disabled college students, the number of institutions that purport to offer the service is increasing.

Critics point out, however, that instructional accommodation for the learning disabled is patently expensive, although failure to provide it could also, in the long run, prove an unwise economy. Critics argue that it is impractical to spend time and energy developing experimental learning strategies on behalf of students whose academic prospects are limited at best. Since learning-disabled students tend to gravitate to learning centers (Pflug, 1973) and learning-disabilities specialists tend to be housed in them, learning centers find themselves at the center of this controversy and again are accused of misaligning their priorities.

Mastery Learning. Mastery learning and its close relative, competency-based learning, are germane to the concept and practice of most learning centers. Their systematized, sequentialized, individualized, and criterion-based orientation places them at odds with the traditional methodologies, to which they pose an alternative. Moreover, their insistence that time is the variable and achievement the constant (Cross, 1976; Roueche and Snow, 1977) is bothersome and even distressing to faculty (Handleman, 1976) and administrators accustomed to grading practices based upon a distribution curve or instructor intuition and accounting systems using semester or quarter time frames. Finally, even those who sympathize with the learning center movement caution that the cost of mastery learning is excessive when compared with more traditional models (Lombardi, 1979a, 1979b), that grades earned with mastery learning techniques may not be equated with grades awarded in a typical instructional situation, and that behavior learned with mastery learning techniques does not possess the integrity of behavior learned in a traditional setting (Hagstrom, 1977). Thus, mastery learning is an issue even within the movement itself.

Credit. Whether a learner should receive credit for competencies or skills attained through an academic support system or mediated means is another issue with some interesting ramifications. Many writers (Cross, 1976; Hertz and others, 1977; McPherson and others, 1976; Peterson, 1975; Roueche and Snow, 1977) have stated the case for award of academic credit. However, some two-year and many four-year institutions do not award credit, arguing that a postsecondary institution should not award credit for "pre-college" skills or that academically different students should not be rewarded for their ineptitude by allowing them to accrue units in grade-credit courses that can be applied to a degree. Notwithstanding research to the contrary, some colleges hold that credits earned in courses making extensive use of instructional media do not possess the value of credits earned in courses that rely on a classroom lecture, instructor-centered methodology. Nevertheless, an increasing number of colleges are now awarding credit for learning skills and "developmental" courses (Cross, 1976), perhaps in an effort to bolster declining enrollment, perhaps in response to the experience of some credit-awarding colleges that have reported better retention rates with high-risk students (Roueche and Snow, 1977).

Affective Cognitive Approaches. Learning facilitators, who are given to innovation and willing to apply learning theories that have substance and promise, were among the first to pilot approaches and methodologies that have aroused the supercilious attention of the academic establishment at large.

Two of these strategies are based upon personality theory;

namely, locus of control and self-concept. Briefly stated, the former proceeds from the notion that the learner who perceives himself as controlling his own destiny is a more successful learner than the individual who perceives his fortune as determined by outside forces, while the latter assumes that a person who possesses a high self-image will be more apt to learn than a person with a low self-image. The practitioner who chooses to apply one or both of these personality theories to the learning process assumes a role that encourages positive attitudes in his clients, chiefly by exposing them to successful learning experiences (Clark, 1980; Drummond and others, 1975), and by caring facilitator behaviors that are calculated to build learner self-confidence and self-esteem (Kirk, 1969; Roueche and Mink, 1976; Spivey and Fleming, 1979). However, critics argue that instruments designed to measure locus of control and self-concept are not sufficiently valid or reliable (Cross, 1976), that there is no strong correlation between locus of control measures and learning ability (Spivey and Fleming, 1979), and that self-concept is not closely or predictably related to academic achievement (Maxwell, 1979).

Two other theories applied in learning centers are based upon cognitive theory; namely, cognitive-style mapping and field dependence/independence. Briefly stated, these theories are based on the assumption that an individual learns best when the particular style or mode of instruction employed is consistent with that individual's identifiable strengths or "preferred style" (Brooks, 1979). Therefore, the learning facilitator helps a client to assess personal learning styles and to match an available mode or style of instructional delivery with the positive features of the student's learning style, taking maximum advantage of learning preferences to enhance motivation and achievement (Clark, 1980; Martin, 1978). However, critics observe that the processes both of identifying learner characteristics and of matching these characteristics with appropriate learning resources is too complicated and time-consuming. Further, they question the practicality of painstaking assessment of students' learning profiles only to find that suitable learning alternatives are not available on campus. Finally, they caution that attempts to adjust to learner idiosyncrasies can even result in overestimation of the psychic fragility of these students (R. Williams, 1971) and encourage an attitude of overassistance that separates students from any realistic conception of the demands of the conventional curriculum (Cross, 1972). Thus, these attempts to employ innovative strategies based upon affective and cognitive theories place learning centers in the midst of controversy.

Staffing. The unorthodox evolution and function of learning centers has occasioned atypical job specifications and duty assignments as well as questionable intraorganizational models. For instance, there is no consistency in the qualifications or credentials of the academic preparation, training, and disciplinary residence for the director of a learning center. Those chosen, recruited, or assigned to that position have come from a variety of backgrounds; sometimes, they assume directorship by default (McPherson and others, 1976; Roueche and Snow, 1977). Given the wide-ranging, multidisciplinary mission of the learning center, which is without precedent, the assignment has been viewed as anything from a refuge for a marginal employee (Moore, 1976) to a residence for an academic renaissance man (Kerstiens, 1972a; Maxwell, 1979). Learning center facilitators and instructors have been depicted both as plodding practitioners engaged in salvage work (Roueche and Snow, 1977) and as conspiratorial innovators threatening to change the academic establishment (Kerstiens, 1972b). Perhaps heretically, Christ views degree and "professional" requirements for these facilitators as essentially inconsequential (Spann, 1979). Learning center professional personnel (tutors, peer counselors, student technicians, classified personnel) are viewed by some as inferiors carrying out the unchallenging routine work prescribed and monitored by a certificated person (McPherson and others, 1976) and by others as adventuresome zealots who accept the responsibility for providing services that previously had been the province of professionals (Mathews, 1971; McPherson and others, 1976). Finally, the team spirit that prevails among learning center personnel who share an advocacy role naturally establishes new working relationships and perceptions of duty that call for organizational and administrative lines of command and parameters of commitment that seem eccentric when compared with traditional models.

Status and Stature. Early in the nineteen seventies academic support systems were regarded as low-grade salvage programs. Typically, these programs were physically and emotionally isolated from the mainstream of the academic community (Kerstiens, 1971). It is clear that, at the time, there were substantive reasons why colleges should perceive a support system as no more than a cosmetic appendage (Jencks and Riesman, 1968). Later writers (Brudner, 1977; Crafts and Gibson, 1975; McClung, 1977) noted that systems for learning assistance as well as systems for the application of media and technology to instruction (Kemp and others, 1980) are still considered extra rather than essential components and that such systems operate on the fringes of academic respectability. However, learning centers persist as an issue that cannot be dismissed.

In fact, since learning centers themselves and their functions are both proliferating, the movement is achieving considerable exposure, if not some creditable recognition. First, since learning centers are commonly considered as an integral part, if not the actual center of, campus developmental studies, they have benefited from the remarkable growth of developmental programs. Next, a growing number of professional publications encourage reports and research on the movement, among them the *Journal of Remedial and Developmental Education, Instructional Innovator,* and the *Proceedings* of the Western College Reading Association. New regional and national associations hold conferences featuring themes related to the movement or its individual features, and in keeping with the trend toward accountability, learning centers are pursuing new research designs to better assess their effectiveness (Clymer, 1978; Peterson, 1974). Finally, learning center personnel are becoming more successful in enlisting the cooperation and participation of departments and other campus agencies (Enright, 1976; Mayfield, 1977; K. Smith and others, 1976) which expands their sphere of influence and increases its diversity.

Future Directions and Emphases

The seeds of the learning center movement have been planted. It appears that only a dramatic change in the nature of the present student population or the total academic ecology can stay its continued development. To hazard a prediction for its growth, we will speculate about some programs, services, and strategies that are still in their early stages.

Leadership in Staff Development. As schools look for ways of accommodating today's learners, whether for egalitarian reasons or the purpose of survival, they recognize that a change in faculty attitudes and behaviors is fundamental. Therefore, we can expect that learning centers will become more involved in encouraging content instruction to incorporate an increased number of learning alternatives into their methodologies; sponsor microteaching sessions or other behavior modification strategies that allow instructors to analyze, and hopefully to improve, their own teaching; organize and lead information sessions at which the latest educational research and innovations can be shared with faculty; coordinate the design and development of instructional programs and modules at special workshop sessions; provide special and expert technical advice to curriculum committees aimed at reshaping the curriculum and its delivery system; lobby for administrative sanction and support of responsible experimentation by enthusiastic faculty while monitoring the project's development and effects; and report the problems and progress of all these endeavors to faculty and other staff in a nonthreatening way that encourages feedback and participation. In each of these roles, learning center directors and facilitators are equipped to be the leaders of change, for they are accustomed to respond to the changing and disparate needs of students upon whom the institution must refocus its attention.

Instructional Innovation and Implementation. We can anticipate that learning centers will multiply their involvement in procuring, producing, and managing individualized learning modules and packages, and that the sophistication, effectiveness, and integration of these materials into a highly accessible, interactive, and interrelated system will increase. As advances in computer-assisted instruction (CAI) allow it to become increasingly interactive and more versatile and cost-effective, CAI will assume its rightful place among the resources that require management. To meet the challenge of managing all these resources, the computer will be exploited inventively, and its software will be redesigned so that computer-managed instruction (CMI) can attain the level of accessibility and individualization required for learners who bear the burden of specialness. Learning centers will continue to refine their applications of cognitive-style mapping and other, as yet undeveloped affective theories. Experiments manipulating instructional time frames and the intensity and focus of special minicourses and microcourses designed to serve special audiences at convenient locations and in appropriate settings will continue. As in other professions, practitioners will become more expert in their use of paraprofessionals, who will assume more responsible and challenging duties as members of an integrated instructional task force. Centers will successfully reverse the misapplications and abuses of instructional television and its relatives the videotape recorder and videodisc, so that this and more humble media will enjoy meaningful versatility, serving mass audiences and individual learners in an interactive system. Above all, learning centers will learn to manage, adjust, and readjust all these components by effecting a marriage of humanism and technology and by developing an evaluation design that will render them accountable.

Institutionalization. Ideally, learning centers will accomplish all of these changes while fulfilling the routine aspects of their mission. If they continue to develop as we have predicted, and if the strategies, methodologies, and programs that they espouse are assimilated by their institutions, learning centers will have so transformed their campuses that there will no longer be a need for learning centers. Learning centers will have succeeded when they have put themselves out of business. Less ideally, learning centers will continue to serve and to protect students as a group and to prod and to push faculty as individuals, making slow headway toward renovation of the college. Under this construction, the learning center will be integrated into the educational system as a constructive critic. Least desirable, if learning centers prove indispensable and are institutionalized for that reason, their existence will no longer be questioned, and they will enjoy the serenity of those academic agencies whose primary goal is proprietary self-perpetuation.

Conclusion

Because learning centers' origins were so diverse, the learning center movement helped bring together psychologists, instructional technologists, English and math instructors, librarians, and counselors. The movement helped coordinate these individuals' efforts to enhance student learning and to make traditional instruction up to date within a facility flexible enough to allow the learning center to become the academic support system for the entire campus community. The learning center, as a relatively new phenomenon, naturally became associated with change, innovation and, consequently, controversy. Under the banner of advocacy—responding to students' real and immediate academic needs—the learning center mission has expanded so that now learning centers are assuming a leadership role in staff development, assisting faculty and staff to improve instruction and more effectively serve students who have learning problems. Therefore, it is in its unity of purpose, youthful vitality, and pluralism of effort that the learning center has found its strength and has deservedly experienced remarkable growth, which promises to continue.

References

Andrews, G. A. "Study Training in the Junior College." *Junior College Journal,* 1932, *2,* (7), 385–389.

Angus, S. "Communication Skills: Promise or Threat?" *School and Society,* 1958, *86,* (2137), 337–338.

Balanoff, N. "James A. Wood Learning Center: A Saturation Experiment at Stephens College." *Audiovisual Instruction,* 1963, *8* (4), 226–229.

Bamman, H. A. "Study Skills Programs, Stanford University." *California Journal of Educational Research,* 1954, *5* (2), 57–58.

Bear, R. B. "Organization of College Reading Programs." *Education,* 1950, *70* (9), 575–581.

Behrens, H. D. "Effects of a How-to-Study Course." *Journal of Higher Education,* 1935, *6* (4), 195–202.

Bergman, I. B. "Integrating Reading Skills with Content in a Two-Year College." *Journal of Reading,* 1977, *20* (4), 327–329.

Blake, W. S., Jr. "A Basic Study Skills Program for Colleges and Universities." *Junior College Journal,* 1955, *26* (3), 164–167.

Blake, W. S., Jr. "Do Probationary College Freshmen Benefit from Compulsory Study Skills and Reading Training?" *Journal of Experimental Education,* 1956, *25* (1), 91–93.

Bock, J. D. "Two-Year College LRC Buildings." *Library Journal,* 1978, *103* (21), 2391–2393.

Bond, J. A. "Freshman Reading Program in Junior College." *Junior College Journal,* 1940, *11* (1), 22–25.

Book, W. F. "Results Obtained in a Special How-to-Study Course Given to College Students." *School and Society,* 1927, *26* (669), 529–534.

Brooks, M. "Nebraska Educational Television Council for Higher Education." *Forum for Reading,* 1979, *10* (2), 3–11.

Brown, E. T. "A Community College's Learning Laboratory." *Wilson Library Bulletin,* 1965, *40* (1), 80–83.

Brown, S., and others. "Technology with Humanism Supports Learning." *Community and Junior College Journal,* 1977, *47* (8), 6–9.

Brudner, H. "The Past, Present, and Future of Instructional Technology in Higher Education." *THE Journal,* 1977, *4* (3), 14–15, 22–26.

Carman, R. A. "Systems Analysis of a Learning Resource Center." Unpublished manuscript, University of California, Los Angeles, 1970. (ED 035 411)

Carpenter, T., and Jones, Y. "Transferring Reading and Study Skills to the Content Area." In W. D. Miller and G. N. McNinch (Eds.), *Reflections and Investigations on Reading: Twenty-Fifth Yearbook of the National Reading Conference.* Milwaukee: National Reading Conference, 1976.

Charters, W. W. "Remedial Reading in College." *Journal of Higher Education,* 1941, *12* (3), 117–121.

Christ, F. L. "The SR/SE Laboratory: A Systems Approach to Reading/Study Skills Counseling." In G. B. Schick and M. M. May (Eds.), *Psychology of Reading Behavior: Eighteenth Yearbook of the National Reading Conference.* Milwaukee: National Reading Conference, 1969.

Christ, F. L. "Systems for Learning Assistance: Learners, Learning Facilitators, and Learning Centers." In F. L. Christ (Ed.), *Interdisciplinary Aspects of Reading Instruction: Proceedings of the Fourth Annual Conference of the Western College Reading Association.* Los Angeles: The Western College Reading Association, 1971.

Clark, R. E. "What Do We Know for Sure?" *Instructional Innovation,* 1980, *25* (1), 28–29.

Clymer, C. "A National Survey of Learning Assistance Evaluation: Rationale, Techniques, Problems." In G. Enright (Ed.), *Learning Assistance — Charting Our Course: Proceedings of the Eleventh Annual Conference of the Western College Reading Association.* Long Beach, Calif.: The Western College Reading Association, 1978.

Crafts, G., and Gibson, A. D. "College Reading Specialists: Are They Being Short-Changed by Graduate Schools?" In R. Sugimoto (Ed.), *College Learning Skills: Today and Tomorrowland: Proceedings of the Eighth Annual Conference of the Western College Reading Association.* Anaheim, Calif.: The Western College Reading Association, 1975.

Cross, K. P. *Beyond the Open Door: New Students to Higher Education.* San Francisco: Jossey-Bass, 1971.

Cross, K. P. *Accent on Learning: Improving Instruction and Reshaping the Curriculum.* San Francisco: Jossey-Bass, 1976.

Cross, K. P. "Education as a Superhighway." *Journal of Developmental and Remedial Education,* 1979, *3* (2), 2–3, 32.

Delong, G. H. "Reading and Study for the Average Student." *Educational Research Bulletin,* 1948, *27* (5), 121–124.

Deterline, W. S. "The Secrets We Keep from Students." *Educational Technology,* 1968, *8* (3), 7–10.

Devirian, M. C., Enright, G., and Smith, G. D. "A Survey of Learning Program Centers in U.S. Institutions of Higher Education." In R. Sugimoto (Ed.), *College Learning Skills: Today and Tomorrowland: Proceedings of the Eighth Annual Conference of the Western College Reading Association,* Anaheim, Calif.: The Western College Reading Association, 1975.

Donisi, P. "The Implications of Closed Circuit Television for Teaching College Reading Courses." In E. P. Bliesmer and R. C. Staiger (Eds.), *Problems, Programs, and Projects in College-Adult Reading: Eleventh Yearbook of the National Reading Conference.* Milwaukee: National Reading Conference, 1962.

Drummond, R. J., Smith, R. K., and Pinette, C. A. "Internal-External Control Construct and Performance in an Individualized Community College Reading Course." *Reading Improvement,* 1975, *12* (1), 34–38.

Durkee, F. M. "Freshman Reading: A Proposed Attack." *College English,* 1952, *14* (1), 30–33.

Eckert, R. E., and Jones, E. S. "Long-Time Effects of Training College Students How to Study." *School and Society,* 1935, *42* (1090), 685–688.

Ellison, J. "Lane Community College Study Skills Center." *Western College Reading Association Newsletter,* Spring 1970, p. 2.

Ellison, J. "The Concept of College and University Learning Resource Centers." Buffalo: State University of New York, 1973. (ED 077 229)

Enright, G. "College Learning Skills: Frontierland Origins of the Learning Assistance Center." In R. Sugimoto (Ed.), *College Learning Skills: Today and Tomorrowland: Proceedings of the Eighth Annual Conference of the Western College Reading Association.* Anaheim, Calif.: The Western College Reading Association, 1975.

Enright, G. "The Study Table and Panic Clinic." In R. Sugimoto (Ed.), *Revolutionizing College Learning Skills: Proceedings of the Ninth Annual Conference of the Western College Reading Association.* Tucson, Ariz.: The Western College Reading Association, 1976.

Enright, G. "A Systematic Program for the Transfer of Learning Skills to the Content Areas." In G. Enright (Ed.), *Proceedings of the Twelfth Annual Conference of the Western College Reading Association.* Honolulu: The Western College Reading Association, 1978.

Fraley, L. W., and Vargas, E. A. "Academic Tradition and Instructional Technology." *Journal of Higher Education,* 1975, *46* (1), 1–15.

Fusario, J. F. "Toward Library College Media Centers." *Junior College Journal,* 1970, *40* (7), 40–44.

Garland, M. "Bill Moore Speaks Out—An Interview with Dr. William E. Moore, Jr." *Journal of Developmental and Remedial Education,* 1978a, *2* (1), 8–9.

Garland, M. "Dr. Roueche, Tell Me: An Interview with Dr. John E. Roueche." *Journal of Developmental and Remedial Education,* 1978b, *1* (1), 5–7, 18.

Gregory, J. W. "An Approach to Functional English in a Four-Year Junior College." *Junior College Journal,* 1958, *29* (4), 203–205.

Gunselman, M. (Ed.). *What Are We Learning About Learning Centers?* Oklahoma City, Okla.: Eagle Media, 1971.

Guskin, A. E., and Greenbaum, B. "Quality and Equality: Basic Skill Requirements at the University Level." *Educational Record,* 1979, *60* (3), 312–318.

Hagstrom, J. "Mastery Learning: The Honeymoon Is Over." In G. Enright (Ed.), *Personalizing Learning Systems—Ecologies and Strategies: Proceedings of the Tenth Annual Conference of the Western College Reading Association.* Denver, Colo.: The Western College Reading Association, 1977.

Handleman, C. "Faculty Members Support 'Back to Basics.' " *Community College Review,* 1976, *4* (3), 42–49.

"Help for the Brightest." *Time Magazine,* February 2, 1976, p. 44.

Henderson, D. D., Melloni, B. J., and Sherman, J. F. "What a Learning Resource Center (LRC) Could Mean for Georgetown University." Unpublished paper. Washington, D.C.: Georgetown University, 1971. (ED 055 417)

Hertz, S. M., and others. "College Credit for Reading Courses—Yes!" *Journal of Reading,* 1977, *20* (8), 688–692.

Hultgren, D. D. "The Role of the Individual Learning Center in Effecting Educational Change." In G. B. Schick and M. M. May (Eds.), *Reading—Process and Pedagogy: Nineteenth Yearbook of the National Reading Conference.* Milwaukee: National Reading Conference, 1970.

Jencks, C., and Riesman, D. *The Academic Revolution.* New York: Doubleday, 1968.

Johnson, A., and Peterson, E. "The Learning Center and the Minicourse." In G. Kerstiens (Ed.), *Reading—Putting All the Cards on the Table: Proceedings of the Fifth Annual Conference of the Western College Reading Association.* Reno, Nev.: The Western College Reading Association, 1972.

Jones, R. C. "Multicampus Instructional Resources Services." *Junior College Journal,* 1966, *36* (6), 11–13.

Kazmierski, P. R. "Affecting Change in College Instruction and Instructors." In D. M. Wark (Ed.), *College and Adult Reading: Sixth Yearbook of the North Central Reading Association.* St. Paul, Minn.: North Central Reading Association, 1971.

Kemp, J. E., and others. "Fads, Fallacies, Failures." *Instructional Innovator,* 1980, *25* (1), 25–27.

Kendrick, S. A., and Thomas, C. L. "Transition from School to College." *Review of Educational Research,* 1970, *40* (10), 151–179.

Kerstiens, G. "Open Enrollment: Challenge to the College Reading/Study Skills Program." In G. B. Schick and M. M. May (Eds.), *Reading — Process and Pedagogy: Nineteenth Yearbook of the National Reading Conference.* Milwaukee: National Reading Conference, 1970.

Kerstiens, G. *Directions for Research and Innovation in Junior College Reading Programs.* Topical Paper No. 18. Los Angeles: ERIC Clearinghouse for Junior Colleges, 1971.

Kerstiens, G. "The Ombudsman Function of the College Learning Center." In F. Greene (Ed.), *College Reading — Problems and Programs of Junior and Senior Colleges: Twenty-First Yearbook of the National Reading Conference.* Boone, N.C.: National Reading Conference, 1972a.

Kerstiens, G. "The Reading-Study Skills Practitioner as Conspiratorial Innovator." *Reading Instruction Journal,* 1972b, *15* (3), 49–50.

Kirk, B. A. "The Relationship of College Reading Programs to Educational Counseling." In G. Schick and M. M. May (Eds.), *The Psychology of Reading Behavior: Eighteenth Yearbook of the National Reading Conference.* Milwaukee: National Reading Conference, 1969.

Knoell, M. *People Who Need College: A Report on Students We Have Yet To Serve.* Washington, D.C.: American Association of Junior Colleges, 1970.

Lombardi, J. "Four Phases of Developmental Education." *Junior College Resource Review.* Los Angeles: ERIC Clearinghouse for Junior Colleges, March 1979b.

Lombardi, J. "Developmental Education: A Rapidly Expanding Function." *Community College Review,* 1979a, *7* (1), 65–72.

McAllister, J. M., Cowgill, S., and Stephenson, J. V. "Why Aren't Your Students Learning?" *Junior College Journal,* 1972, *42* (6), 24–26.

McCarthy, M. M. "Court Cases with an Impact on Reading." *Journal of Reading,* 1979, *23* (3), 205–211.

McClung, C. "Back-to-Basics a Threat to the Field?" *THE Journal,* 1977, *6* (5), 52.

McGann, M. "Improving the Scholarship of College Freshmen with Remedial Reading Instruction." *Journal of Educational Psychology,* 1948, *39* (3), 183–186.

McPherson, E., and others. *Learning Skills Centers: A CCCC Report.* Urbana, Ill.: ERIC Clearinghouse on Reading and Communications Skills, 1976.

Martin, R. G. "Cognitive Therapy: A New Mission for Community Colleges." In M. Marty (Ed.), *New Directions for Community Colleges: Responding to New Missions,* no. 24. San Francisco: Jossey-Bass, 1978.

Mathews, T. "Twenty Days in August: An Intensive Program." In F. L. Christ (Ed.), *Interdisciplinary Aspects of Reading Instruction: Proceedings of the Fourth Annual Conference of the Western College Reading Association.* Los Angeles: The Western College Reading Association, 1971.

Maxwell, M. *Improving Student Learning Skills: A Comprehensive Guide to Successful Practices and Programs for Increasing the Performance of Underprepared Students.* San Francisco: Jossey-Bass, 1979.

Mayfield, C. K. "Establishing a Reading and Study Skills Course for Law Students." *Journal of Reading,* 1977, *20* (4), 285–287.

Meierhenry, W. C. "Instructional Theory: From Behaviorism to Humanism to Synergism." *Instructional Innovator,* 1980, *25* (1), 16–18.

Merren, J. "A Catalog of College and University Learning Centers." *Audiovisual Instruction*, 1975, *20* (9), 15–23.

Merrill, I. R., and Drob, H. A. *Criteria for Planning the College and University Learning Resources Center*. Washington, D.C.: Association for Educational Communications and Technology, 1977.

Moore, W., Jr. *Community College Responses to the High Risk Student: A Critical Reappraisal*. Washington, D.C.: American Association of Community and Junior Colleges, 1976.

Morgan, W. E. "Junior College Developments in California." *The Junior College Journal*, 1930, *1* (2), 64–68.

Neidt, C. O. "Use of a Videotaped Instructional Television for Teaching Study Skills in a University Setting." *A.V. Communications Review*, 1967, *15* (3), 263–284.

Newman, L. "Remedial Reading in the Junior College." In M. P. Douglass (Ed.), *Beyond Literacy: Thirteenth Yearbook of the Claremont Reading Conference*. Claremont, Calif.: The Claremont Reading Conference, 1966.

Park, Y. "A Conceptual Basis for Nontraditional Study." *Community and Junior College Journal*, 1976, *46* (6), 29–31.

Parr, F. W. "The Extent of Remedial Reading Work in State Universities in the United States." *School and Society*, 1930, *31* (799), 547–548.

Peterson, G. T. "Conceptualizing the Learning Center." *Audiovisual Instruction*, 1973, *18* (3), 67, 70, 72.

Peterson, G. T. *An Analysis of the Learning Center in the Community College*. Concord, Calif.: California Association for Educational Media and Technology, 1974.

Peterson, G. T. *The Learning Center: A Sphere for Nontraditional Approaches to Education*. Hamden, Conn.: Lennet Books, 1975.

Pflug, R. J. "The Handicapped and Disadvantaged Students in the Learning Center." In G. Kerstiens (Ed.), *Technological Alternatives in Learning: Proceedings of the Sixth Annual Conference of the Western College Reading Association*. Albuquerque, N.M.: The Western College Reading Association, 1973.

"A Question of Malpractice." *Change*, 1978, *10* (7), 8–9.

Raygor, A. L., and Summers, E. G. "Progress in Programmed Instruction." In A. Raygor (Ed.), *College and Adult Reading: Second Annual Yearbook of the North Central Reading Association*. Minneapolis: University of Minnesota, 1963.

Reger, R. "Futile Attempts at Simplistic LD Definitions." *Journal of Learning Disabilities*, 1979, *12* (8), 529–532.

Robinson, F. P. *Effective Study*. New York: Harper & Row, 1941.

Robinson, F. P. "Two Quarries with a Single Stone." *Journal of Higher Education*, 1945, *16* (4), 201–206.

Roueche, J. E. *Salvage, Redirection, or Custody? Remedial Education in the Community Junior College*. ERIC Clearinghouse for Junior College Information Monograph Series. Washington, D.C.: American Association of Junior Colleges, 1968.

Roueche, J. E., and Pitman, J. C. *A Modest Proposal: Students Can Learn*. San Francisco: Jossey-Bass, 1972.

Roueche, J. E., and Mink, O. G. "Helping the 'Unmotivated' Student: Toward Personhood Development." *Community College Review*, 1976, *4* (4), 40–50.

Roueche, J. E., and Snow, J. J. *Overcoming Learning Problems: A Guide to Developmental Education in College*. San Francisco: Jossey-Bass, 1977.

Saettler, P. "The Roots of Educational Technology." *Programmed Learning and Educational Technology*, 1978, *15* (1), 7–15.

See, S. G. "Implementing the Learning Resources Center." In G. Kerstiens (Ed.), *Reading Update — Ideals to Reality: Proceedings of the Seventh Annual Conference of the Western College Reading Association*. Oakland, Calif.: The Western College Reading Association, 1974.

Sharp, S. L. "Effective Study Methods." *Journal of Higher Education*, 1943, *14* (5), 271–272.

Shaughnessy, M. P. *Errors and Expectations—A Guide for the Teacher of Basic Writing.* New York: Oxford University Press, 1977.

Simpson, R. G. "The Reading Laboratory as a Service Unit in College." *School and Society,* 1942, *55* (1431), 621–623.

Smith, G. D., Enright, G., and Devirian, M. "A National Survey of Learning and Study Skills Programs." In G. McNinch and W. D. Miller (Eds.), *Reading—Convention and Inquiry: Twenty-Fourth Yearbook of the National Reading Conference.* Boone, N.C.: National Reading Conference, 1975.

Smith, K. G., Clymer, C., and Brabham, R. D. "Revolutionizing the Attitudes of Academia Through a Learning Skills Center." In R. Sugimoto (Ed.), *Revolutionizing College Learning Skills: Proceedings of the Ninth Annual Conference of the Western College Reading Association.* Tucson, Ariz.: The Western College Reading Association, 1976.

Spache, G. D., and others. "College Reading Programs." *Journal of Developmental Reading,* 1959, *2* (4), 35–46.

Spache, G. D. "College-Adult Reading—Past, Present, and Future." In G. B. Schick and M. M. May (Eds.), *The Psychology of Reading Behavior: Eighteenth Yearbook of the National Reading Conference.* Milwaukee: National Reading Conference, 1969.

Spann, N. C. "Interview with Frank Christ." *Journal of Developmental and Remedial Education,* 1979, *3* (1), 8–11.

Spivey, N. N., and Fleming, D. R. "Locus of Control: An Important Student Variable in the College Learning Center." In G. Enright (Ed.), *Proceedings of the Twelfth Annual Conference of the Western College Reading Association.* Honolulu: The Western College Reading Association, 1979.

Sullivan, L. *A Guide to Higher Education Learning Centers in the United States and Canada.* Portsmouth, N.H.: Entelek, 1978.

Sullivan, R. J. "Learning Disabilities in College: The University Role." *Journal of Reading,* 1975, *19* (1), 6–7.

Suppes, P., and Macken, E. "The Historical Path from Research and Development to Operational Use of CAI." *Educational Technology,* 1978, *18* (4), 9–11.

Suppes, P., and Morningstar, M. "Computer-Assisted Instruction." *Science,* 1969, *166* (3903), 343–350.

Swindling, J. A. "Attitudes of Community College Instructors Toward Reading: A Process for Change." In G. Enright (Ed.), *Personalizing Learning Systems—Ecologies and Strategies: Proceedings of the Tenth Annual Conference of the Western College Reading Association.* Denver, Colo.: The Western College Reading Association, 1977.

Tomlinson, B., and Tomlinson, M. D. "Integrating Reading and Study Skills into College Biology." In W. D. Miller and G. H. McNinch (Eds.), *Reflections and Investigations on Reading: Twenty-Fifth Yearbook of the National Reading Conference.* Clemson, S.C.: National Reading Conference, 1976.

Touhey, J. F. "The Learning Center: Its Role and Future Implications for the Junior College." Paper presented to the International Reading Association, May 1970. (ED 042 586).

Tresselt, M. E., and Richlin, M. "Differential Prognosis in a College Study Methods Course." *Journal of Psychology,* 1951, *31,* 81–89.

Triggs, F. O. "Remedial Reading Programs: Evidence of Their Development." *Journal of Educational Psychology,* 1942, *33* (9), 678–685.

"TV Retention and Learning." *School and Society,* 1958, *86* (2136), 323–324.

Von KleinSmid, R. B., and Touton, F. C. *Effective Study Procedures in Junior College and Lower Division Courses.* University of Southern California Studies, Educational Series No. 8. Los Angeles: University of Southern California, 1929.

Walker, C., and others. "A Learning Assistance Center at Stanford?" In G. Kerstiens (Ed.), *Reading Update—Ideals to Reality: Proceedings of the Seventh Annual Conference of the Western College Reading Association.* Oakland, Calif.: The Western College Reading Association, 1974.

Walker, G. H., Jr. "Remedial Reading Programs in Negro Colleges and Universities." *Journal of Negro Education,* 1946, *15* (1), 119–121.

Watson, N. E., and Luskin, B. J. "Cables, Cassettes, and Computers at Coast." *Junior and Community College Journal,* 1972, *43* (3), 12–13.

Weber, C. B. "An Experimental Course in Remedial Writing." *Junior College Journal,* 1954, *24* (5), 285–291.

Whipple, G. M. *How to Study Effectively.* Illinois: Public School Publishing Company, 1916.

Williams, G. "Use of the Computer for Testing and Programming in a Reading Program." In G. B. Schick and M. M. May (Eds.), *Junior College and Adult Reading Programs, Expanding Fields: Sixteenth Yearbook of the National Reading Conference.* Milwaukee: National Reading Conference, 1967.

Williams, G. "Editor's Comment." *Western College Reading Association Newsletter,* Spring 1971, p.1.

Williams, R. "The New Sentimentality." A commencement address delivered at Western Washington State College, Bellingham, June 11, 1971.

Wittenborn, J. R. "Classes in Remedial Reading and Study Habits." *Journal of Educational Research,* 1944, *37* (8), 571–586.

Witty, P. A. "Practices in Corrective Reading in Colleges and Universities." *School and Society,* 1940, *52* (1353), 564–568.

Woolley, J. "A Study of Tutorial Services Offered in California Community Colleges." Unpublished doctoral dissertation, Brigham Young University, 1976.

Zerga, J. E. "Remedial Reading Programs." *Junior College Journal,* 1940, *11* (4), 194–195.

Gwyn Enright is director of the Independent Learning Center at San Diego City College; editor of the WCRA Proceedings; *and has designed and developed learning centers in both two-year and four-year institutions of higher education.*

Gene Kerstiens is associate dean, Learning Resources at El Camino College. He has served as president, Western College Reading Association; editor, WCRA Proceedings; *advisory editor, the* Journal of Reading *and the* Journal of Developmental and Remedial Education; *and has developed audiotutorial learning modules in English, reading, and academic skills used in higher eduction learning centers.*

No matter how hostile the faculty may at first appear,
proponents of learning centers can use negotiations
over credit as a way of engaging the faculty in
activities that serve all students and,
ultimately, all faculty as well.

Learning Centers and the Faculty: Improving Academic Competency

James W. Shaw

The attitude of faculty toward learning centers might be characterized as opinionated ambivalence: They are not sure that there really is a problem. If there is, they are not sure that universities ought to take on the responsibility of solving it. They know that they do not like any of the proposals that they have heard so far. If you pin them down, they doubt that learning centers should be established. However, if learning centers are established, they do not want anyone else to run them, although they do not want to run them themselves.

Anyone who senses such attitudes would no doubt be wary of involving faculty in the development of a learning center. This is precisely what has happened on most campuses. Support for the kind of basic teaching done by learning centers has come from academic administrators, student affairs staff, and even students—everyone but the teaching faculty. This has compromised the very concept of learning centers, not to mention their goals, structures, methods, and effectiveness. Clearly, learning centers cannot prevail in the face of faculty opposition or even sufferance; if they are to succeed in the teaching mission they have ascribed to themselves, they must enlist the full political and pedagogical support of the professional teaching staff.

Can this be done? If faculty are truly people who "think otherwise," it may seem likely that they will prefer that someone go ahead and institute a learning center in spite of them, so they can feel free to criticize the entire operation on procedural, jurisdictional, and pedagogical grounds. This is not the case. Although faculty may appear to be perverse in their responses to new ideas, the response is one conditioned by 800 years of institutionalized questioning, dating back to the medieval "disputation"—defense of a thesis by any new student seeking certification to teach. Like these students, learning centers are new. Like these students, they are candidates for certification to teach. As a result, the burden of proof lies on them, not with them. By mistaking questioning for opposition, many proponents of learning centers have insulated themselves from faculty—potentially their best allies.

Is There a Problem?

Paradoxically, the faculty's ambivalence toward the issue of whether there indeed is a problem is also the opportunity for a mutually helpful alliance.

On the one hand, faculty sometimes feel that there is no problem whatsoever. True, some students come poorly prepared, but, aside from the difficulties that they pose for the teachers of introductory courses, they are a self-correcting problem: They flunk out. In this sense, they are less a problem than a fact of academic life: Some people should not be in college. We may even take some comfort from the fact that, although it has long been held that only half of the nation's high school graduates enter college and that only half of the entrants finish, current statistics indicate that as many as 60 percent of the entrants eventually are graduated. The seeming acceptance of such a "success" ratio does not mean, as some within academic institutions infer, that faculty are oblivious to social needs and unsympathetic to students as individuals. On the contrary, it means that faculty maintain the same primary allegiance to the truth in their role of certifying agent that they maintain in their roles of researcher and teacher. To certify that a student cannot do calculus is as much a service both to society and to the individual as to certify that a student can. Thus, when faculty assert that there is no problem, they are not maintaining arbitrary standards, as some would have it, but accepting the unpleasant truth that everyone has limitations and that some people discover theirs in college.

On the other hand, faculty ambivalence shows up when they not only admit but volunteer that a problem exists: Too many students are simply not well enough prepared to take advantage of what is offered in classrooms. However, faculty always seem to be complaining that their students are not as good as they used to be, as if the entire history of higher education had been a steady decline since the University of Bologna's class of 58 — 1158, that is.

Thus, while many faculty believe that severe learning problems probably cannot and in some cases should not be treated, because treatment will only postpone the inevitable, they are also aware, often as a result of their own successful interventions on behalf of "diamonds in the rough," that many students, like many soldiers, can be led where they cannot be driven. Accordingly, the proponent of learning centers who advocates them as a cure for retention problems, or — worse — who takes the approach that any student can be salvaged, will be looked upon by faculty as naive at best. But the proponent who advocates the establishment of a center to relieve faculty of teaching things that "should have been taught in high school" will at least get a sympathetic hearing and perhaps also some actual support.

Should Colleges and Universities Assume Responsibility?

I am not claiming that accepting the faculty definition of the problem will guarantee an alliance, for even when faculty acknowledge the existence of a problem, they remain ambivalent about the advisability of assuming responsibility for solving it. That is, if the problem originates in the high schools, it should be remedied there. Again, this should not be deprecated as hardhearted elitism; more than likely, it is a common sense acknowledgement of the limitations of individual faculty and of the college or university as a whole. Few faculty teach well at all levels — introductory, advanced, and graduate. To add still another level could invite professors who are not proficient to rush in where even professionals fear to tread. Similarly, colleges and universities cannot be all things to all people. Indeed, they are finding it increasingly difficult to be even the special thing that they are intended to be. To ask that they add new functions when they cannot master existing ones is to endanger their credibility even further. Often, however, the wish of faculty to avoid responsibility for treating learning problems is not so high-minded. Not principle but avoidance characterizes the response: Yes, there is a problem, but it is not to be solved on campus but off campus — by the admissions office. If the admissions office found better students, then faculty would not have to face the question of whether postsecondary institutions should treat learning problems.

There is also a psychological dimension to the question. From the faculty's point of view, the very concept of a learning center contains a threat: the implication that if faculty were doing their job properly, a learning center would not be necessary. As much as they cherish their position at the apex of the educational hierarchy and as often as they assert that they should not spend time teaching what others were supposed to teach, the suspicion remains that they either cannot or will not do such teaching. One needs only to note the mutual recriminations voiced by teachers of introductory and graduate courses to sense how thorny such issues of relative competency can become. Moreover, faculty have the examples of previous failures to warn them from doing anything that could invite criticism. For example, the failure of many of the residential colleges established in the late nineteen sixties was caused in no small part by the indifference or hostility of the old-line faculty, not coincidentally the same faculty in reaction to whose curriculum and teaching methods these innovations had been set up. Similarly, courses sponsored by student affairs agencies have had to fight for survival, not simply because the teachers of these courses lacked traditional academic credentials (even the Ed.D. is suspect in the eyes of many faculty) but also because these courses were designed and advertised as remedies for the deficiencies of the regular faculty's offerings. In short, the psychological dangers of even seeming to compete with professionals in their own expertise cannot be overestimated.

Even more important than a wish to deny that a problem exists, a desire to place the responsibility for solving it elsewhere, or defensiveness about the attempts of others to solve it is the philosophical conviction held by most faculty that universities should not be engaged in "remedial" work.

Remedial is a taboo word. It names a reality we may acknowledge but wish not to utter. Indeed, even the proponents of remedial work are loath to call it that, and the euphemism *learning center* is worrisome too. In any case, we wish to avoid the inference that "learning centers" do "remedial" work. Instead, we advocate the establishment of "skills centers," which can take students "where they're at" and provide "academic support services" to "special, exceptional, academically disadvantaged, or culturally deprived persons" who, we hope, will profit from the "learning options" offered in these "alternative education programs."

In a compassionate effort to avoid stigmatizing the students for whom these services are provided, to avoid being pejorative, and perhaps also to head off impassioned attacks from the faculty, who seem to oppose the whole idea, universities have adopted a language that obscures what proponents of such services are trying to do and misleads opponents, clients, and even colleagues.

Is what we are talking about "remedial" work? Yes. By definition, clients of learning centers lack (or feel that they lack) competencies which they should (or feel that they should) already possess. Literally, learning centers provide "remedies," which either "redress" the omission of a first exposure or "relieve" the pain of an incorrect exposure. Measured on some absolute scale of intellectual health, clients may not be sick at all, but measured against their peers, they seem to suffer from a debilitating disease, and it is the charge of the learning center to restore them to a state of health.

The issue of remediation is important not because it is crucial to the supporters of learning centers—it is not: learning centers have a whole spectrum of work to do, regardless of what one segment of that work may be called—but because it is crucial to those who oppose the very existence of learning centers. If the teaching is not remedial, then everyone can agree that it belongs in the college and university, that it should be done by regular faculty, and that traditional modes of teaching will suffice. For example, departments of foreign languages teach and give credit for introductory and intermediate courses which their students could have elected in high school; English departments offer courses in rhetoric or freshman English in which elementary-school grammar, junior high reading skills, and high school-level critical thinking are taught; and most mathematics departments teach some form of pre-precalculus. Yet such teaching has not been defined as remedial.

But what if certain teaching is remedial? Does it belong in the college or university?

Faculty ambivalence on this point has become truly academic. Demography makes cowards of us all! That is, even if admissions offices do a better job, the smaller clientele for postsecondary education may mean our staying the same. College and universities which conclude that they cannot or should not address learning problems may find that students will choose institutions which can and will. Faculty who feel unqualified for such teaching may find that there are no others to perform the task—or, worse, that there are. Thus, however unsure we may be about the advisability of colleges and universities undertaking the charge represented by learning centers, we may be sure of the necessity.

Yet it is unsatisfactory, both philosophically and politically, to resolve the issue in such mundane terms. Grudging tolerance is hardly the best mandate from the faculty, and a mandate from any other source provokes faculty opposition on grounds of space, jurisdiction, and budget. All these practical considerations can be managed and political support can be won if the proponents of learning centers reach a measure of philosophical agreement with faculty on one issue, credit.

To Credit or Not to Credit

Of all the issues that learning centers raise for faculty, credit is the most troublesome. Faculty recognize and accept that many others in a college or university are also engaged in "eduation" and that many others also "teach"; what distinguishes faculty from all others engaged in education is the privilege of awarding credit. Hence, to credit or not to credit is even more important for faculty than it is for students, since assigning credit defines who is and who is not faculty.

Although such concern for credit may appear to others to be merely defensive on the part of faculty, the concern is one which everyone associated with a college or university must share. Credit is the coin of the realm, and if everyone is allowed the right of coinage, then the currency becomes debased, a kind of inflation sets in, and the confidence of the outside world, so essential to our survival, erodes. To credit says that we are willing to stand behind our promises. Thus, it would be cynical to believe that personal interest is the only thing at stake here. Faculty are, above all, idealists, and the ideal which binds them together is the search for truth. In this context, the decision to credit is an issue of telling the truth about whether someone else possesses the truth.

Accordingly, in the eyes of the faculty credit is not a reward but a kind of right. They feel that it should not be promised as an inducement to enroll but that it should be conferred in recognition of the attainment of a certain level of truth. This twofold belief lies at the root of most conflicts between faculty and the proponents of learning centers.

Some proponents, whom we can call the pragmatists, feel caught in a dilemma. They do not believe that the activities of a learning center should be credit-bearing. In effect, they accept the faculty criterion—the attainment of a certain level of truth—and they feel that however many "new" truths their clients acquire, these truths lie below the level acknowledged by crediting. Nonetheless, they recognize that many, if not most, of their potential clients will ignore the help available in learning centers unless that help carries credit. Pragmatically, they seek credit in order to have students to teach.

How accurate the assumptions of the pragmatists are is debatable. First, the assumption that students will not avail themselves of help unless it is credited is not an either/or issue, for on every campus students engage in activities that are educationally good, true, and beautiful but do not always yield credit: tutorials, debate teams, publications, public service, internships, peer counseling, and bull sessions with older, sadder, and wiser compatriots. Even on campuses where some of these activities do yield credit, it is seldom true that the continued existence of the activity depends on that alone. Conversely, there are other activities—grammar, vocabulary, basic math—in which students will engage only because credit is awarded, and even they seem to do so with reluctance. Perhaps most perplexing for the pragmatists is the fear that the students most in need of help are those least disposed to seek it: special admissions students whose financial aid is predicated upon the completion of eight full-time semesters of study, students whose basic problem is their view of education as a cash-and-carry operation in which the aim is to get most goods for the least expense, and ordinary students who will not subject themselves to the stigma inflicted by noncourses. In fact, it often seems as if the only students willing to pursue uncredited learning are those who need it least, the superior students who characteristically pursue every opportunity. Thus, the danger for pragmatists lies not in assuming that a problem exists but that the problem is pervasive or that credit is the only answer. There are other, proven ways of motivating students, not the least of which is the antiestablishment appeal of useful learning packaged in something other than one-hour-a-day, three-days-a-week units, and there are other options for breaking out of bureaucratic constraints. Faculty will at least expect a pragmatist to show that all other alternatives have been exhausted.

The second assumption made by pragmatists is that the end justifies the means. Even if students can only be led to the good and the necessary by the awarding of credit, does this justify the award? Faculty, of course, will argue that it does not. However desirable it may be to remedy certain educational deficiencies, it is even more desirable to maintain truth and to certify or validate only genuine educational achievement.

The third assumption held by pragmatists is perhaps the most disturbing, for it puts them in conflict not with others — the faculty — but with their own colleagues — those other proponents of credit for the work of learning centers, the developmentalists. Whereas pragmatists grant not only that credit should be conferred only as a recognition of the attainment of a certain level of truth but also assume that much of the learning that takes place in learning centers is below the creditable level, developmentalists believe that the idea of level itself is misleading and that what should be credited is progress. The crucial issue is thus joined: Is credit to be awarded for process or for product?

Those who argue for progress or process make two telling points: first, that product or level is so variable throughout the academic community as to be almost meaningless and, second, that if anything is creditable, growth certainly must be.

Any faculty can be shamed almost into silence by the developmentalist who points to certain courses in the curriculum and asks, "Where are your standards now?" Basketweaving, potmaking, and the philosophy of football are damaging enough, but, even worse, faculty know where the other bodies are buried — Professor X's long-dead course in one department, Professor Y's grading standards in another, and the very existence of department Z. Again, what level of truth is certified by the award of a D grade? Even the worst learning center can prove itself superior to such standards as these. Further, if it is true that virtually all colleges and universities compile roughly the same grade point averages and offer the same degrees, what can quality control possibly mean? In short, developmentalists assert, there is no level of truth justifying the award of any credit.

The dangers in this line of argument are obvious. Pedagogically, no learning center wishes to be measured against the lowest common denominator. Politically, no faculty will be so bound by precedent as to replicate its most egregious errors. Other dangers may be less obvious. Only a pyrrhic victory is gained if faculty are persuaded that a learning center is only the equal of something they already disdain, and on top of that it is only temporary, given the inevitability of reform movements. Finally, to assert that no standards exist will be perceived as not only negative but wrong. Some consensus about the level of truth required for credit does exist in academe, and the embarrassing exceptions only serve to underline the rule.

A far more positive and appealing argument is that of the developmentalists, who assert that growth itself is creditable. Moreover, there is not a faculty member alive who has not at some time or other acted (albeit guiltily) on that premise, giving a student a D for attendance or a C for effort on the assumption that the student is better now than when he or she entered the course. In fact, the guilt that a faculty member may feel for deserting standards is tempered by the sheer pleasure of dispensing a reward, for, while it may not be better to give a good grade than to receive one, it is good enough. Part of the pleasure derives, of course, from the faculty member's acute awareness of the strong influence that rewards exert on motivation. In fact, some faculty seem to know of no other motivation than grades and credits. In short, faculty know at first hand the pleasures and the pedagogical soundness of rewarding progress. Of course, they also know the dangers.

These dangers threaten everyone: the teacher, the student, and the outside world. For the teacher, the danger lies in the ease of rewarding growth; every student can show some. In awarding credit for progress, the faculty member ceases to discriminate—a function which is central to good pedagogy. Truths and even skills may be acquired at a variety of levels, but this vanity is not infinite; at some point the teacher has the obligation to tell the student that a truth or a skill has not yet been acquired, no matter how much progress has been made.

For the student, the danger lies in being deluded. The credit is no substitute for the truth or skill. Students ask, trust, and even demand of us that we tell them when they "know." Schools are now being sued for having falsely assured students that they did "know." The ethical indictment is even more onerous. A faculty member has one ultimate responsibility to the student—not to guide, not to encourage, not to support, but to tell the truth and thus to help in a unique way. This is to say that faculty should not reward process—they do so, psychologically, all the time—but that they defraud their students if they confuse process and product for their students by assigning equal "credit" to each.

The danger for the outside world is related to the danger for teachers and students. If every student progresses, then does every student not also deserve credit? If so, what value does credit have? Students wish to be certified so that the outside world will recognize them as having certain competencies. Students and the outside world trust faculty to use grades, credits, and degrees to do this. If faculty certify process as if it were product and growth as if it were proficiency, then faculty have compromised themselves, their students, and society. None of us wants to be operated on by a surgeon who has shown good progress in surgery. In a word, while faculty believe that growth should be rewarded, credit is not necessarily the proper reward.

Negotiating with Faculty

Does this perspective leave any grounds for rapprochement? Yes. The fact that faculty are reluctant to credit what they perceive to be remedial work means only that what is to be credited must be negotiated.

The criteria that faculty bring to such negotiations have little to do with learning as a process but much to do with learning as a product. Normally, that product is knowledge. Skills, the very raison d'être of the learning center, are viewed by faculty as a means to an end, namely the acquisition of knowledge, not as an end in themselves. The role played by laboratories in science courses is representative; although more time may be spent in the lab than in the classroom, lab exercises usually count as only one fifth or one sixth of the grade and yield only one of the four credits awarded. Similarly, writing courses, which very obviously are skill-oriented, are usually termed "Principles of Rhetoric" or "Elements of Persuasion" than "Techniques of Exposition" or "Organizational Skills." Internships furnish perhaps the best illustration. Although they clearly teach students many kinds of how-to skills—how to analyze a probelm, how to identify resources, how to synthesize information, in a word, how to cope—only recently and reluctantly have these activities been credited by faculty.

The main criterion that governs faculty thinking in making distinctions between the creditable and the noncreditable is often hidden—not intentionally but because faculty by nature or conditioning have come to assume it. This criterion is abstraction. Virtually any course that yields or at least manipulates abstract concepts is virtually assured of accreditation. Although faculty are often accused of denigrating the practical, in reality most faculty place such high value on abstraction precisely because they see it as being more practical than applied studies.

An awareness of this benign bias can be helpful to proponents of learning centers in two ways. First, an alliance with faculty should begin in one area of agreement: courses that emphasize abstraction. Thus, a course in learning how to learn might best be called "Theories and Principles of Learning." The end product of such a course would not be a mere skill but an infinitely applicable body of knowledge. Second, in the case of courses that faculty flatly object to crediting, addition of units providing abstract understanding will probably win support. Philosophically and tactically, then, mutual interest in broadly applicable principles of learning is a bridge between knowledge and skills.

I do not mean to imply that faculty acceptance in the form of credit will ever come easily. Ironically, the closer the content of the teaching done in learning centers comes to the content of teaching done in the regular classroom, the less likely are faculty to approve credit, for, because it is provided in a learning center, such content is by definition subdisciplinary. Of course, the proponents of learning centers can always invoke the necessity mentioned earlier: retention problems, the lack of faculty qualified or interested in back-to-basics teaching, and the desire of faculty to have their courses pitched at a level at which they wish to teach. Necessity, however, will not overcome faculty concerns about subdisciplinary content. Proponents of learning centers would thus be wise to avoid forcing the issue of credit for subdisciplinary teaching and learning. Instead, they should focus on crediting nondisciplinary or interdisciplinary teaching and learning. A writing skills course that incorporates linguistics, cognition, persuasion, and logic will seem — and be — multidisciplinary and thus capable of providing new abstractions as well as traditional skills.

If the proponents of learning centers can use such approaches to negotiate successfully with faculty on credit, a symbolic bridge will have been built. More than anything else, credit can represent the community of interest which exists between learning centers and faculty. Faculty, after all, have no intrinsic reservations about learning centers. Their overriding concern is for competency, both among students and teachers. Once that issue is settled, the others will fade. In fact, if it is handled properly, the very process of negotiating criteria for the award of credit can be the best possible vehicle not only for involving faculty in the development of a learning center but also for enlisting their continuing political and pedagogical support. Once they have been reassured on the crucial issue of credit for remedial work, faculty are free to consider on merit all the other desirable functions of learning centers.

Faculty Involvement

Of course, to maintain faculty support requires as much courage and patience as it does to gain it. First, the director of a learning center should seek to establish a faculty advisory committee. True, the cost in time and trauma of dealing with such a committee is high, but the rewards are substantial. At the very least, since individual committee members probably embody representative points of view, they can function as an early warning system against potentially harmful criticism. Further, each member brings expertise in a given field and can therefore function in any operation, their advice can complement an insider's view and thereby head off many kinds of mistakes. Often, consultants become converts for no other reason than their familiarity with the actual accomplishments of an organization. Politically, such allies are invaluable.

Ideally, such an advisory committee would include members from as many disciplines as possible. To lie outside all departmental influence is to be isolated, but to be subject to the influence of a single department is to be controlled or to run the risk of satisfying one constituency at the expense of others. A writing program that satisfies only the English department will probably fail to satisfy both business and engineering. However, a program that is guided by representatives of the English, mathematics, education, psychology, and statistics departments and the professional schools will not only generate broadly based support by avoiding a narrow disciplinary view but will also profit from having such a variety of lobbyists at budget time. In fact, jointly sponsored budgets are virtually immune to cutting because each contributor's stake is so small while each one's benefit is so great. An administrative and budgetary home in the liberal arts college is the most desirable because it automatically transforms the center director from one of "them" into one of "us."

Finally, and perhaps most importantly, significant pedagogical and political advantages are to be gained if the learning center is quite broadly defined. Pedagogically, by offering testing, measurement, research, tutorials, modules, classes, counseling, and teaching to everyone — not only marginal admissions but graduate students writing theses — a learning center can fulfill its unique mission of responding to students' individual needs. Politically, the best case for tenure has always included teaching, service, and research. By involving faculty in all of these functions—especially a research component—the learning center can become fully integrated into the life of the university.

Future Roles and Relationships

What would full integration of faculty and learning centers mean? Can such an ideal, mutually supportive relationship exist? Theoretically it can, though whether local needs, traditions, ambitions, and competencies will allow it to exist is another question.

Basically, learning centers seem destined to evolve into agencies that serve all students, in a way that supplements and thus supports the traditional teaching performed by faculty. This projection is based upon two assumptions, namely that the role of the faculty as teachers is likely to remain traditional and that there are a large number of other educational services which both students and teachers want someone to provide.

As pedagogically and politically important as it may be to involve faculty in the activities of a learning center, it is not likely that such involvement will convert faculty to the kinds of teaching that learning centers do. Even when faced with the phasing out of existing positions and the opportunity to retrain for new positions, faculty—by training and inclination if not by ability—are reluctant to abandon their traditional teaching roles for the kinds of teaching done in learning centers or, for that matter, for any remarkably different kind of teaching. In fact, what little evidence we have seems to suggest that even among the youngest and most adaptable of Ph.D.s, attrition occurs more often than adaptation; that is, it seems likely that more recent English Ph.D.s are learning to drive cabs than to teach economics or K-12 English. The implications of such behavior are, first, that few faculty are likely to teach in learning centers and, second, that most faculty will continue to teach traditional subjects in traditional ways, despite the importunities of students, administrators, and trustees. Critics are apt to view this as evidence either of imperceptiveness or of resignation—the academic equivalent of the band that continues to play as the Titanic slips beneath the waves. However, in some sense it is simply an affirmation of faith in the eternal verities, in this case the liberal arts tradition. Academe has weathered so many storms—secularization, professionalism, the free elective system, learning by doing, vocationalism—and coped with so many kinds of new clients—the laity, women, veterans, the counterculture, minorities, and older students—while maintaining enrollments in a basic curriculum not remarkably different from the trivium and the quadrivium that faculty must be granted the benefit of the doubt when they assert that many of these verities are, indeed, eternal. In short, neither learning centers nor even the so-called new students whose educational needs they represent are likely to transform what or how faculty teach.

This is not to denigrate learning centers or to limit their functions; if anything, it enhances them. If, as our second assumption implies, the need and demand for different educational services increases and if the faculty continues to function traditionally, then it follows that these new services must be provided by someone other than faculty — presumably by learning centers. For this reason, the role of learning centers in supplementing and thus supporting the traditional teaching role of the faculty should remain uncontested. As long as they supplement rather than compete with the faculty, their status should be secure.

As we have seen, to supplement this role means to assume responsibility for research and noncredited or credited but nondisciplinary teaching. Fortunately for the proponents of learning centers, these "other" educational services are so valuable that virtually all faculty can support them and so various that virtually all students can draw upon them. In fact, there are at least three of these supportive services that both students and faculty want someone to provide, especially in view of the fact that faculty will not or cannot provide them.

The first of these is determining a student's readiness for a given course or curriculum. Something more sophisticated than the rough measures employed by the admissions office and the advising service is needed, as the large number of requests for late drops, incompleteness, and even expungements of failures shows. This is not to suggest that admissions and advising staff are inept at reading scores and transcripts but rather that no one can possibly know how to interpret a B earned in phase 4 of intermediate precalculus at West Utopia High School and Community College and still less how well it may parallel the local version of advanced beginning calculus. An increasing number of faculty are designing their own entrance examinations, not to govern admission to the college but to their own courses. They tend to design poorly. A few sample problems or a few sample vocabulary exercises administered during the first week of the course are always inefficient and often inadequate. Instead, both faculty and students want some process for determining — in fact, for certifying — that a student is prepared for the content that will be presented.

Ideally, this process would be more than a test. It would involve a measure of knowledge and skills, an estimate of raw ability, an evaluation of motivation and sophistication, a projection of how people with similar profiles fared in various sections, and an analysis of potentially dangerous yet remediable weaknesses. Only a learning center possesses the capability for such thorough assessment. Of course, not all students and courses could be assessed in this way, but certain problem-prone students and courses could be identified and offered the service.

The second service commonly requested by students and faculty alike is diagnostic testing. Students often perceive that they are doing poorly, but they do not know why. Faculty perceive that their students are doing poorly, but they cannot discover why. In fact, faculty can labor under the double disadvantage of understanding the difficulties of their subject too well and the difficulties of their students too little. Someone with time and expertise is needed to diagnose the problem and prescribe a remedy. Again, only a learning center can explore the many factors that can cause a student to do poorly, factors which neither the student nor the teacher may be able to name.

The third service that students and faculty request of learning centers is, of course, the treatment of learning difficulties. In addition to mounting abstract, non- or multidisciplinary courses in conjunction with regular faculty, learning centers can draw upon various kinds of nontraditional resources and options. Consequently, we might expect to see learning centers lead the way in the use of new kinds of teachers and new kinds of teaching. Learning centers will be free to hire under-credentialed or differently credentialed teachers; to contract with these teachers for specific time periods, skills, and even results; to extend the movement begun with peer counseling and peer advising to peer teaching; and to redefine the role of teaching assistant, which heretofore has meant someone who, whatever his or her function, would never presume to offer faculty any true assistance with their teaching. Similarly, learning centers will need to develop approaches to teaching which by definition transcend the classroom: tutorials, modules, self-paced learning, interactive programs—approaches from the highly individualized to the broadly generalized. In effect, learning centers should function as a sort of avant-garde library or resource center, and they will be confirmed in that role if they share space with the library. As always, learning centers will find it advantageous to work with faculty, in this case as a proving ground for prototypes of new kinds of teachers and new kinds of teaching.

Finally, it is not too farfetched to imagine a day when learning centers will engage in that most suspicious of all activities in higher education, teaching teachers. Indeed, learning centers will find their greatest opportunity to enhance learning in this activity. Once faculty have gained confidence in the ability of the learning center to help their students, it is only a short step to point out that the learning problem may lie not with the student but with the teacher or, more tactfully, with the teaching. Most attempts at improving the teaching on college campuses have failed, either because they were tied to evaluation of teaching or rewards for teaching or because they existed in a situation where the improvement had no practical consequences. The learning problem of a student referred to the learning center is already a practical consequence of something that has transpired in the classroom. When learning centers themselves have learned to communicate solutions not only in terms of students but also of teachers, we will be near the millenium; it will be upon us when the faculty as well as the students come for help.

Conclusion

In summary, difficult as the initial relationships between the learning center and the faculty may be, a positive relationship must exist between them if the center is to realize its potential. This means that the faculty must be engaged rather than avoided, and the best point of engagement is the one with the greatest symbolic importance, credit. The understanding and accommodation necessary to resolve problems associated with credit can provide the basis for a mutually supportive alliance in which learning centers earn the faculty's pedagogical and political support by supplementing and thus supporting traditional classroom teaching. Ideally, a learning center should neither ignore nor compete with faculty, but should educate them to become collaborators and even clients.

James W. Shaw is associate dean of the College of Arts and Sciences at the University of Massachusetts, Amherst, where he teaches in the Department of English, and a past president of the National Association of Academic Affairs Association.

*While the college learning center has traditionally served as a
laboratory for exploring innovative instructional/curricular
methods and sometimes as a catalyst for instructional
improvement, it has the potential for serving as an agent for
change in campus-wide instructional/curricular practices.*

Learning Centers and Instructional/Curricular Reform

June Dempsey
Barbara Tomlinson

A number of factors have enabled college learning centers and their
staffs to make distinctive contributions to the improvement of instruction and curriculum: experience in changing institutional and instructional patterns while establishing the learning center, an emphasis on
how concepts are learned as well as on *which* concepts are learned, a
focus on the individual and on the individualization of and accountability to students as well as to administrators. While we cannot expect
that any curricular change will enable all students at a particular college to achieve success, learning center staff can help their faculty colleagues develop curriculums better adapted to the learning climate of
their institution and to the abilities and strategies of their students.

Learning Centers as Change Agents

Learning center staff have often functioned as change agents
while organizing and developing new learning assistance programs
within their institutions. In establishing a strong and successful learning center program, they respond to a sense of a need for change in the

curriculum; diagnose the problems of two client systems, students and faculty; assess the capacity of those systems to change; examine their own motivations and resources for bringing about changes in learning behaviors and academic performance; establish good working relationships with both client systems; examine alternative goals and instructional routes toward those goals; select the alternatives appropriate to their institution, client systems, and resources; formulate and carry out specific plans for change; evaluate the effects of the change; and generalize and stabilize the change. These steps in the development of new and growing learning centers parallel several models that describe planned change as an interaction between change agents and client systems (Buchanan, 1967; Lippitt and others, 1958; National Training Laboratories, 1966) compared in Louis M. Maguire's *Observations and Analysis of the Literature on Change* (1970). Whether acting as catalysts for change by encouraging awareness of student learning problems, as solution-givers by proposing curricular innovations to reduce those problems, or as process-helpers by contributing to faculty curricular development, the learning center staff can offer special insight into college instructional improvement.

Emphasis on Process Learning

Because learning center programs frequently teach skills in preparation for classes in various academic disciplines, much of the center's curriculum concentrates on helping students learn how to learn—through reading, through writing, through studying and problem solving. One major contribution of the learning center to curricular improvement is its focus on how a discipline may be learned, rather than on the information and concepts that must be understood for success in the discipline. Many successful learners, including most teachers, may not realize that teaching focused on the concepts and information that are the products of learning is, in effect, assumptive teaching—teaching which assumes that the student knows what activities lead to the desired product and how to go about completing those activities successfully. Assessing course demands and providing curriculums that bridge the gap between student skills and course demands frequently become the province of the learning center. In a given discipline, there are two groups of people who may know how to learn in that discipline: faculty in that discipline, who have learned how to learn and think like chemists, historians, or philosophers, and learning skills specialists, who have learned how students acquire and manipulate concepts. By applying their understanding to student course materials, learning center staff construct process curriculums.

Verbalization of Process. One method that has been used to teach the learning process is the verbalization method (Whimbey,

1977), which allows instructors who are experts in analyzing the concepts particular to a discipline and in practicing the best way to learn them, to demonstrate their techniques to the learner. These instructors think aloud while working through ideas or problems, vocalizing their thoughts as relationships are analyzed, concepts are sorted, and generalizations are formed. Research indicates that verbalizers exhibit enough of their thinking processes to enable observing students to follow their mental paths through problem solving or the acquisition of complex concepts. Students are encouraged to emulate these processes by verbalizing their own thinking, mimicking their instructors as they work on problems of their own while being monitored and assisted by the instructors. The University of Houston is using this method in study labs for a course in analytical reading and study skills. There are courses using the verbalization procedure at other universities as well (Whimbey, 1977).

Adjunct Classes. Another method for teaching process strategies in the learning center setting is adjunct class programming. Adjunct classes integrate reading, writing, or study skills instruction with the content of an academic course. Such integration enhances opportunities for immediate improvement in grades, since the processes taught address the demands of the correlated academic course; develops motivation for changing strategies, since the skills taught are immediately accessible, relevant to the student's learning concerns, and tested in the heat of battle; reduces the need for transfer of training, since the skills are taught in the setting where they must be utilized; and habituates the student to the new strategies, since regular practice of each technique is included in the course.

While the adjunct class uses many or most of the materials required in the academic course with which it is integrated, its goal is to develop skills and to encourage the transfer of skills to other coursework through acceptance, internalization, and habituation. Adjunct class instruction may be provided by a member of the learning center staff who specializes in the study skills required for a particular discipline or by a team composed of a subject matter specialist and a learning specialist, but the instruction must not be concerned with the subject matter of the correlated academic course to the detriment of the process strategies that are the proper focus of the adjunct class. When academic instructors choose to teach learning skills as part of their own activities, they must learn to step outside their involvement with the material of the class in order to deal with the student's learning processes. Further, they must pay particular attention to the processes that will be useful to the naive student who is not gifted with the instructor's special love or understanding of the discipline.

The curriculum of the adjunct class may be organized to suit the goals of an institution, a learning center, or an academic course. Some curriculums, such as those at the University of California at Riverside and at Irvine (Tomlinson and Greene, 1976; Tomlinson and Tomlinson, 1976), develop reading and study skills needed for success in correlated courses; others, such as the adjunct programs at Metropolitan State College in Denver that develop Piagetian formal operations thinking, attempt to influence the cognitive strategies needed for successful completion of the correlated course; others, such as the writing adjunct classes at California State University at Dominguez Hills correlated with specific courses in other academic disciplines, provide skills activities in related areas; and still others, such as the independent study materials developed at San Diego City College (Enright, 1979), provide content modules that combine learning skills strategies with background concepts important for an understanding of the content of the correlated course. Curriculums may be based on a survey of student concerns; problem areas identified by instructors; tutors, or learning center staff; or a task analysis of the techniques needed by students to complete the course successfully. In some institutions, the adjunct class functions as a credit course that parallels another credit course, with the student being enrolled in both courses. In other institutions, adjunct classes are noncredit but required support classes for students who fail to meet normal entrance requirements or to maintain acceptable grades. Other colleges utilize adjunct programming flexibly, as voluntary ongoing noncredit classes, workshops, or self-help programs. The correlated development of process skills and content understanding achieved by adjunct programming is a powerful tool for the improvement both of instruction and student academic performance.

Attention to the Individual

Directors of learning centers have generally heeded the admonition that their programs must have well-publicized, clearly defined goals. It would be difficult to find a learning center that did not list assistance to individual learners as one of its primary goals. This goal may be stated in a variety of ways: to help students learn to learn, to help students gain self-confidence, to help students improve their self-concepts, to help students overcome their learning anxieties, to provide individualized assistance, to help students achieve their academic potentials, or to serve as an ombudsman for students on campus with problems. No matter how it is worded, the goal focuses on individual learners in all aspects of their academic lives. Centers are usually designed so that students can be addressed as individuals when they have not learned well in the group instructional settings found in most colleges.

Skills Development. The original learning assistance program model emphasized instruction in general reading and studying skills. The models now emerging, however, include flexible class formats, small-group work, individual counseling and tutoring, and self-help programming in a variety of areas, all incorporated into center curriculums in response to the needs of the individuals requiring help. The following list identifies some of the skills that individual students have needed in order to succeed in their course work.

1. *Reading:* Comprehension, rate, flexibility, critical analysis, reading in specific content areas, vocabulary development, study-type reading.

2. *Study Skills:* Time management, concentration, concept mapping, outlining, listening and notetaking, test anxiety reduction, studying for specific content areas.

3. *Writing:* Organization, style, grammatical usage, logic, writing processes, writing anxiety reduction, writing in specific content areas, writing for publication.

4. *English as a Second Language:* Listening, speaking, writing, reading in practical, social, and academic settings.

5. *Critical Thinking:* Questioning, inference, analysis, synthesis, formal operations, problem solving, cognitive style.

6. *Qualifying Exam Preparation:* Test-taking strategies, mathematics review, verbal review, test anxiety reduction.

Centers may engage in diagnostic assessment of student reading, writing, and study skills, problem-solving strategies, cognitive style, and educational background. Frequently, an individual program will be prepared for the student, indicating a development plan for strengthening skills, in which the student is deficient. While the center's curriculum often involves individualized instruction in one form or another, the skills development of individual students does not require individualization; a program that supplies appropriate group activities that meet the individual student's needs also demonstrates respect for personal differences.

Affective Factors. The focus on the individual learner in many learning centers includes attention to the attitudes, anxieties, and psychological influences that inhibit or even preclude successful learning for many students. For this reason, many centers adopt a counseling as well as a didactic role and provide supportive counseling on changing habits, setting goals, managing time and stress, adapting to cognitive style, and gaining control of one's learning. To be successful, learning skills counseling requires empathy, a flexible approach, intuition in discussion and diagnosis, insight into diverse academic disciplines, and sensitivity to students' felt needs as well as to observed needs. Personal counseling accompanied by warmth, understanding, and acceptance encourages students to reveal concerns and deficiencies that they might continue to conceal in a more formal classroom environment; often, real progress toward overcoming learning deficiencies cannot be made until these concerns, problems, and failures are addressed. The experience of learning centers suggests that a system of personal support can spell the difference between success and failure in attempts to alter learning performance.

Learning centers may adapt grading strategies or curriculums in order to address affective considerations. To provide low-anxiety settings that will enable students to feel free to explore changes in learning strategies, centers use a variety of grading techniques. While not uniformly positive, the grade-free environment of learning skills programs in some colleges and universities does enable involved students to learn without the stress which accompanies grades. Voluntary participation in learning skills programs ensures that most students will be self-selected, highly motivated, and concerned with skills development rather than earning a high grade. Those who hold to the view that it is inefficient, and perhaps even immoral, to allow students to pursue an academic road to a destination of failure recommend that students whose diagnoses predict almost certain failure bé required to receive learning assistance — as much for their own sake as for the institution's. Those who support required programs generally recommend that credit be granted for classes designed to alleviate the academic deficiencies of the ill-prepared (Roueche and Snow, 1977). In general, the grading practices of learning centers tend to place the needs of the invividual above those of the institution. Their experiences with alternative grading practices may contribute useful information to institutions on the pedagogical implications of grading within their various instructional programs.

Learning centers have also attempted to address affective issues directly, by developing curriculums that integrate counseling with skills development. Programs to reduce anxiety about learning are one example. Often, the components on anxiety reduction in study skills courses directly concern attitudinal problems, such as those which result from learned helplessness (as in the case of many women when dealing with mathematics) and from "learned failure" (as in the case of underprepared students). Materials and sessions that deal with the reduction of anxiety are frequently found in programs to aid students in preparing for tests and taking tests, math skills preparation, and preparation for professional and graduate school entrance examinations (Dellans, 1979). Math clinics, where students can receive "first aid" for "mathophobia" are springing up around the country (Tobias, 1978), usually in college or university learning centers. The approach used by these math clinics goes beyond mere review and remediation. Instead, they provide a learning situation in which tensions are lowered because instructors make no prior assumptions about their students' mastery of basic math skills and directly discuss fears that arise in the instructional situation. In combination, skills development, enhanced self-confidence, and group support enable individual students to face and deal with their academic fears. In the future, components designed to reduce student's fears about learning and being tested will be included in regular academic courses, and anxiety-reducing materials will be developed for use with individuals and groups. In the case of anxiety-reducing activities, attention to individuals' affective needs has led to changes in group instruction.

Individualization of Instruction

The term *individualized instruction* has been used by many, and they have differing aims and ideals, but the one thing they have in common is a respect for the differing aptitudes of each student, a respect for the impact of ability, background, and style on individual learning performance. The goals set by the various individualized instructional programs fall along a continuum ranging from bureaucratic adaptations for individuals at one end to full-blown student-selected and organized curriculums at the other. Learning centers use modular scheduling, self-paced modules, or programmed instructional materials to change the time structures required for the completion of certain basic or supplementary courses. Sometimes the learning facilitator acts as a program designer, assigning available materials to individual students to obtain an enhanced match to their achievement level, motivation, and learning style or assigning appropriate work in flexible groups or minicourses. To achieve real independence and self-directed learning in their students, many learning centers that work with students on a voluntary basis allow them to make important instructional self-assessments and curriculum decisions and to function as true partners in the learning task.

Since the learning center is often the major mode for delivery of individualized instruction on a campus, learning skills instructors have been instrumental in encouraging campus-wide consideration of individualized instruction in both content and skills areas. Their focus on each student's unique set of knowledge, attitudes, and skills implies continued use and refinement of diagnostic procedures, supportive counseling, alternative instructional modes, independent learning practices, modified timetables for completion of assignments, and student selection of learning experiences. An overview of some of the individualized instructional strategies used in learning centers follows.

Modular Scheduling and Self-Paced Modules. In many academic areas, instruction has been held to the traditional semester or quarter time frame by the belief that all students must cover all aspects of the course, generally at the same pace. Even advanced placement tests are purportedly designed to measure whether a student has mastered an entire subject. Math and vocational technology have used modular teaching for some time, but it may be a while before educators in other disciplines recognize that a student may need to learn only some aspects of a course because other aspects have been learned previously. Diagnostic tests to measure knowledge of specific aspects of a conceptual area will need to be developed. Matched achievement tests will indicate areas subsequently mastered. These tests can then serve to guide instruction. Of course, teachers will have to be willing to explore new ways of managing and delivering material through alternatives or supplements to regularly scheduled lectures. Learning specialists can offer invaluable assistance to academic instructors in each of these areas: diagnosis of student competence, use of appropriate methods for providing information to students, organization and delivery of material, and evaluation of learning.

The use of self-paced modules, introduced after it was recognized that students learned at different rates, indicates an acceptance of the idea that the length of time spent in learning is not necessarily a measure of the degree of mastery (Cross, 1971). Without ignoring the problems created by flexible time frames for the award of credit, proponents of self-paced mastery learning affirm that it is one of the most effective methods of instruction for low achievers (Cross, 1971; Lewis, 1964). Others feel that there is little evidence to support the lofty claims that it is a panacea for the underprepared (Hagstrom, 1977; Maxwell, 1979). Since many centers include mastery learning modules in their programs, facilitators can explore their practical effectiveness for teaching and learning skills by conducting and reporting research on modules that they use for various purposes within alternative curriculums.

Flexible Grouping and Self-Instructional Materials. The desire to individualize instruction in the learning center does not always imply the construction of a package of independent study self-instructional materials which the student utilizes in isolation. Many centers develop individually assigned curricular components as small, fluid subgroups composed of students drawn from one academic class, from sections of a larger class, or from the campus as a whole. Because of the learning center instructor's limited time investment both in preparation and in delivery, small-group programs can provide a place for experimentation, creativity, and innovation. Groups may focus on expressed or intuited student needs. For example, when each writing class section has only a few students who show persistent problems in a grammatical area or organizational subskill, as is often the case, it becomes both pedagogically and financially feasible to form a small instructional group of those students. Students from all the sections of the composition program attend a supplementary workshop. This ensures that the intensive help they need does not impede the progress of other students in their sections. At the University of California at Irvine, student subgroups in writing skills courses have addressed such topics as "Getting Started (Prewriting Techniques)," "Pronoun Reference and Subject-Verb Agreement," "Writing the Comparison-and-Contrast Paper," "Technical Writing for Electrical Engineering," "Essay Test-Taking," "Vocabulary Development for Paper Writing," "Writing a History Term Paper," "Writing on Plato," "Writing a Lab Report," "Dissertation Writers' Support Group."

Minicourses, short-term programs relating to different academic areas or appealing to different student populations, enable the learning center staff to provide some very specific help to a wide variety of students without the expenditure of time required for an ongoing class or for individual counseling. At San Jose State University, minicourses are offered several times a week by advanced sign-up, last between one and two hours, and focus on one study skill, such as notetaking or time scheduling (Spaulding, 1975). Thus, students can select to learn what they need to know without being required to take an entire course. "Problem Solving for Chemistry" or "Preparing for Finals in Humanities" can be provided by centers with limited resources and staff to help students reconsider their study strategies. At Ohlone College in Fremont, California, a variety of minicourses was prepared on video cassette. Some are used to train tutors, who then assist students enrolled in the learning center. Others are designed to introduce a self-paced individualized course and to demonstrate its materials, equipment, and assignments. Still others deal with individual study skills and are used informally by students and instructors (Maloney, 1975). Such a flexible structure may be a desirable addition to current strategies, which teach all students similar or identical content without choice by the student.

The computer-assisted instruction found in a number of learning centers may be typical of programmed and self-instructional curriculums. While falling short of educators' expectations, students' anticipations, and technologists' predictions, computer-assisted instruction, with branch programming to provide supplementary information, offers potentially attractive avenues for individualization of instruction. The best-known programs were developed for science and math instruction, but De Anza College in Cupertino, California, has been piloting a spelling course for college students, and the University of California at Berkeley is developing computer-assisted writing improvement programs. It will be interesting to see whether learning specialists can devise ways of overcoming the problems associated with computer-assisted instruction: high cost, inadequate prepared content, the limited number of relevant commercial programs, and students' boredom and feelings of isolation. The potential of interactive programs in both informational and effective areas may be very great. In any case, computer assistance in instructional management—in diagnosis, placement, supplemental instruction, and record keeping—is also valuable. For several years, De Anza College has been using a computer analysis of individual's test scores to match them with appropriate levels of instructional materials. The computer is also used to keep a record of the students' activities in the instructional program. Learning specialists need to obtain more information on the cost and efficiency of current computer-assisted programs and to explore ways that will allow these programs, and the associated costs, to be shared by many campuses.

Whether learning facilitators choose flexible grouping or self-instructional materials, they are aware that the individualizing of instruction means selecting the approach and material according to the learner's characteristics and needs (James, 1975). Flexibility, which continues to be the key to individualization, may help instructors outside the learning center improve the ability of their classes by teaching to those characteristics and needs.

Flexibility of Format and Curriculum

For some years, learning assistance centers have been providing instructional help to students in a variety of formats, times, locations, levels of difficulty, and topics. Formats may include semester- or quarter-long courses meeting two or three times weekly; late-starting semester or quarter courses; credit, noncredit, and variable-credit courses; ongoing minicourses of several sessions starting at staggered times through the semester; open-entry/open exit courses which students may begin when interested and leave when minimum course requirements are completed; self-help lab courses in which students contract to complete specific tasks; single-session workshops which focus on a specific discipline; and individual counseling/instructional sessions. Innovative formats have been used for a number of years by community colleges in their attempt to reach diverse student populations. Such adjustments may also be appropriate in the curriculums of more traditional four-year colleges and universities.

Flexibility of time and location also characterize many learning center programs. Learning center personnel are frequently the first to arrive on campus in the morning and the last to leave at the end of the day. While colleagues may resent and resist the notion that weekend classes might help to open up educational opportunities for those who cannot attend courses offered during traditional hours, learning skills specialists provide courses, workshops, and sessions on weekends and in the late afternoon and evening. For example, Delta Community College, in Stockton, California, arranged study skills courses for teacher's aides of one school district on selected Fridays and Saturdays in accordance with the district's inservice schedule. Many other colleges and universities have scheduled special courses for selected students in unusual locations: police and fire stations, hospitals, trailer parks, community centers, senior citizen centers, libraries, public schools, and dorms. The energy crisis and the opening of education to nontraditional groups may cause colleges and universities to consider offering traditional courses also in these unusual sites. And once again, the campus learning center will have provided a solution worthy of emulation.

It is not to the advantage of the learning center to have a good reputation only for dealing with poor and remedial students, because the center can offer assistance even to able and high-achieving students, and the resulting mix of abilities might serve to attract poor students who were reluctant to participate in center activities because they feared being stigmatized. Faculty are also much more likely to incorporate learning center staff and programs into their planning when they discover that these programs can also contribute to the success of good students. Many current learning center programs are not designed solely for remedial students: learning center activities range from instructing adult students in community colleges in basic literacy skills so they can obtain employment to teaching university graduate students about writing and time management skills so they can complete dissertations of high quality. Rather than tracking such students, the learning center provides flexible programming, which allows students to track themselves according to need.

Programs intended to aid both superior and remedial learners may have to go beyond the courses in speed reading and qualifying exam preparation presently offered on many university campuses. One solution may be the development of credit classes that integrate theoretical information about learning skills with practical application of the theories. Two courses offered at the University of California at Irvine exemplify this approach. "Applied Reading Theory" introduces and analyzes theories and research in reading that relate to the process of mature reading. Students consider psycholinguistic, developmental, communications, information processing, and sociolinguistic theories of reading, as well as patterns of text organization. Course assignments require students to apply these theories as they analyze the reading process in themselves. "Applied Learning Theory" introduces and analyzes theories and research in areas of learning, memory, communication, and critical thinking that contribute to effective learning at the college level. Students are expected to demonstrate their ability to apply these theories to their own academic learning problems. These two courses have attracted and maintained the interest both of superior and remedial learners. The University of Oregon's credit-bearing "Introduction to University Study" incorporates the teaching of reading and study strategies into a course that develops student understanding of the theory and philosophy of the university. The course addresses the history and growth of higher education, the origins and functions of the university, the goals of the research institution, and the bases for establishment of the university curriculum; each topic has correlated study skills assignments. Both strong and weak students are able to develop learning skills in this class, and students emerge from it with an awareness of their own purposes within the structure of the university.

Accountability to Students

The learning center's concern for student accountability, which is imposed on it both by program mandate and by philosophy, demands that the curriculum be designed to meet the needs of individual learners with flexibility and specificity. The center often attempts to serve students as a refuge from the impersonalization of campus policies and personnel, yet its staff also feel the need to provide students with accurate, and sometimes painful, information about their skills deficiencies. The resulting dilemma for the learning counselor requires that center evaluation policies be at once thoughtful and frank. Students with a history of academic failure are often fearful of evaluation, uncertain of the criteria by which they will be evaluated, unable to pull from brief teacher comments the information they need for effective learning, writing, or test taking, and unable to apply such information to actual learning and assessment situations if they have it. As a result, learning centers must develop a low-key method of evaluation that is based on criteria carefully analyzed by the instructor and made explicit to the student. Evaluation should also be thought of as positive comments to students about specific methods which they can follow to improve problem areas and comments that will provoke student-to-student and student-to-teacher discussions about applying these methods to the next learning or writing situation. Evaluation of this nature, focused as it is on future growth, is an appropriate part of all academic evaluation, but it is particularly appropriate to the learning center, which is accountable to students for their time and effort. The relief with which many students receive this type of evaluation and their frequently expressed enthusiasm for the success which results from it suggests that the use of evaluation and feedback strategies in broader instructional settings is a good idea.

Campus-Wide Collaboration on
Instructional Improvement

The individualized, flexible, process-focused nature of learning assistance instruction and its capacity for integrating the concerns and curriculums of many academic disciplines make it a strong vehicle for promoting a campus-wide effort to improve instruction and curriculum. The fact that learning skills centers evaluate their own staff and programs, often correlate their programs with work in particular courses and disciplines, and serve students who have not been successful in traditional classes naturally leads them to a concern with the evaluation of courses, curriculums, and instructors. Learning center personnel may assist evaluation aimed at course improvement by providing insight into student learning processes. Center staff have developed a special point of view because they work intimately with students who are failing to understand, remember, and manipulate course concepts under the current instructional formats. Center staff also have an impression of the total scope and impact of large courses taught by many teaching assistants, because they interact with students from many class sections. Further, students are often quite frank about their perception of the effectiveness of a given curriculum when they are seeking learning skills help to master its concepts. Frequently, then, learning center staff are in a position to describe to faculty the nature of the problems that students who are not learning well under current teaching and curricular structures are having. This in itself is a valuable contribution.

However, the learning center staff cannot be experts in every academic discipline. What they have to contribute is, rather, their flexibility, their expertise in exploring, understanding, and addressing learning, reading, and writing strategies, and their understanding of how new curriculums can influence and be influenced by those strategies. As a rule, learning center staff are also not experts in instructional improvement itself. Nevertheless, since in many cases the learning center is an innovation within the institution by virtue of its very creation and development, center staff have obtained a good deal of practical experience in the selection, implementation, and evaluation of curricular change.

Establishing Good Working Relationships. In *The Politics of Educational Innovation,* Ernest House (1974) emphasizes that most innovation is dependent on face-to-face personal contacts and that these contacts condition the occurrence and frequency of innovation. In the curriculum of the total institution, the learning skills program is often considered an innovation. As a result, acceptance for it depends on face-to-face contact. Good relationships should be established with faculty members at the center's inception, since they are the basis for any further contributions to institutional teaching improvements. Learning skills staff should meet with faculty groups and individual faculty members to discuss the organization and focus of center programs and their relationship to the activities of particular academic disciplines and classes. Close referral relationships must be established when many students from certain large departments or classes choose to use learning assistance programs. That is, since freshman classes, writing classes, and rigorous math and science courses produce a disproportionate number of students desiring learning skills help, many centers find it effective to have a liaison attend the faculty meetings of those courses to ensure that center staff are familiar with the philosophy and the demands of those departments and that the departments are fully aware of center philosophy and support programming. Faculty from departments with strong referral relationships should be involved in all committees for hiring professional learning skills staff—even part-time temporary staff. Incorporating faculty from outside the center into hiring committees increases confidence in the center; faculty know that the center staff is strong because they have helped to select it.

Personal contact that establishes a climate for innovation is fostered also by more formal curricular relationships. Adjunct classes and workshops establish credibility with faculty members who see immediate improvement in students attending learning programs. At the request of faculty, or of students with faculty approval, learning center staff may produce adjunct materials supporting a particular course syllabus. Such materials develop understanding of background concepts implicit in course instruction, such as algebraic manipulation for basic chemistry courses or topic probing for paper writing in history classes. Reciprocal training allows both academic faculty and learning center staff to benefit. Learning program staff can provide information to teaching assistants and to faculty members about teaching improvement in such areas as organizing and delivering efficient lectures, assigning and grading term papers to promote good writing as well as good topic coverage, developing effective essay test questions, and preparing overview materials and questions for reading assignments. Faculty can provide information to learning center staff about their own research and teaching specialties as they relate to such issues pertinent to center programming as cultural characteristics of student ethnic subpopulations, new developments in transformational grammar, new experiments in learning, and new learning theories. Trust between learning center staff and faculty of other departments will develop as the center seeks campus acceptance for its own programs to improve instruction. Such trust is essential if the center is to contribute to campus-wide instructional improvement.

Change Agent Role. In his *Guide to Innovation in Education,* Havelock (1970) notes three roles that can be assumed by an educator who functions as an agent-for-change-catalyst, solution-giver, and process-helper. The very existence of the learning center, with the consequent development of new support programming and integrative teaching, can serve as a catalyst for change if it sparks an interest in other faculty members about the ways in which their students acquire and manipulate information. Frequently, center staff are informed about new methods for teaching and structuring curriculums as they attempt to meet the needs of students who have difficulty under current instructional methods. If they provide information on these new methods to faculty, they are functioning as solution-givers. But it is as process-helpers that center staff can contribute most strongly to instructional and curricular change. The role of the process-helper includes:

- Showing the client how to recognize and define needs
- Showing the client how to diagnose problems and set objectives
- Showing the client how to acquire relevant resources
- Showing the client how to select or create solutions
- Showing the client how to adapt or install solutions
- Showing the client how to evaluate solutions to determine if they are satisfying his [or her] needs (Havelock, 1970, p. 7).

When functioning as process-helpers, center staff do not supply the content on which the process works—that is done by faculty specialists in the discipline, who well understand the material and concepts they wish to teach—but a process by which successful control of these concepts can be achieved.

As process-helpers who have experience in change strategies and who participate in the activities of many academic disciplines as improvers of skills, learning center staff can contribute to campus-wide instructional improvement in at least six ways.

1. They can help other instructors determine the goals of their courses in terms of both behavioral and intangible objectives.

2. They can help other instructors diagnose the teaching/learning problems of their current classes, whether those of group instruction or individual learning, and set objectives for curricular change which may solve the problems.

3. They can help other instructors to develop, obtain, and adapt materials and tutors that will further their instructional goals.

4. They can help other instructors consider the range of available solutions and assess their suitability for meeting the goals of a given course and for solving the instructional problems delineated.

5. They can help other instructors implement and fine-tune their curricular changes.

6. They can help other instructors to evaluate whether the instructional changes have, in fact, influenced student performance and attitudes and furthered course goals.

However, since learning center staff frequently see themselves as somewhat isolated from instructors in "regular" disciplines (they often lack faculty appointments, despite qualifications fully equal to those of "regular" faculty), they may underestimate their ability to influence curricular reform. House (1974) notes that innovative changes are successful when there is a small group of people who advocate the innovation and provide support for an individual entrepreneur or themselves acting as an entrepreneurial group. Group "solidarity," a "cohesive viewpoint," and the development of a sense of "mission" are fostered when the entrepreneurial group comes from an educational area which is not fully established. "The areas trying to 'make it' educationally and academically would be the most active" (House, 1974, p. 64). Mayhew (1976) believes that educators who attempt to make substantial changes are those who are somewhat peripheral in their institutions, which enables them to consider potentially threatening alternatives, but still be integrated enough to be effective. In fact, he states that "the phenomenon of marginality is an important element leading to innovation" (p. 15). Thus, House and Mayhew both lend support to our contention that the special role of the learning center within the institution makes it a likely force for fostering curricular and instructional change.

Conclusion

It seems clear that both from their roles within the institution and from the activities they perform to fulfill those roles, learning center staff are particularly qualified to act as change agents — contributors to instructional improvement. They are influenced in their roles as learning facilitators, curriculum designers, and curriculum evaluators by the knowledge and attitudes that they have developed in the learning center setting — a setting that emphasizes process as opposed to product learning, students as individuals, individualized instruction, flexibility and variety of format and curriculum, and accountability to students. Their experiences in developing learning centers, which by their nature must respond to needs for new and revised curriculums, further enhance their ability to contribute to instructional change. The process for solving instructional problems that starts with the establishment of a learning center involves diagnosis of specific curricular needs, acquisition of relevant resources, selection or creation of solutions to problems, implementation of new programs, and concern for evaluation. These processes are completed by center staff as they attempt to combine the personality and problems of an individual institution and its students with theoretical and curricular information available from outside the institution. Many learning centers have had to define themselves and their objectives within the structure of their college or university. For this reason, their staff members are often good agents for stimulating change in others because they themselves have had to change. The learning center staff thus possess a unique constellation of skills, which they can draw upon in working collaboratively with faculty for campus-wide improvements in instruction and curriculum.

References

Buchanan, P. C. "Crucial Issues in Organizational Development." In G. Watson (Ed.), *Change in School Systems.* Washington, D.C.: Cooperative Project for Educational Development, National Training Laboratories, National Educational Association, 1967.

Cross, K. P. *Beyond the Open Door: New Students to Higher Education.* San Francisco: Jossey-Bass, 1971.

Dellans, M. "Math Anxiety: What Can a Learning Center Do About It?" In G. Enright (Ed.), *Proceedings of the Twelfth Annual Conference of the Western College Reading Association.* Honolulu, Hawaii: The Western College Reading Association, 1979.

Enright, G. "A Systematic Program for the Transfer of Learning Skills to the Content Areas." In G. Enright (Ed.), *Proceedings of the Twelfth Annual Conference of the Western College Reading Association.* Honolulu, Hawaii: The Western College Reading Association, 1979.

Hagstrom, J. "Mastery Learning: The Honeymoon Is Over." In G. Enright (Ed.), *Proceedings of the Tenth Annual Conference of the Western College Reading Association.* Denver, Colo.: The Western College Reading Association, 1977.

Havelock, R. G. *A Guide to Innovation in Education.* Ann Arbor: Center for Research in the Utilization of Scientific Knowledge, Institute for Social Research, University of Michigan, 1970.

House, E. *The Politics of Educational Innovation.* Berkeley, Calif.: McCutchan, 1974.

James, B. "Self-Paced Instruction—Is It Really Individualized?" In R. Sugimoto (Ed.), *Proceedings of the Eighth Annual Conference of the Western College Reading Association.* Anaheim, Calif.: The Western College Reading Association, 1975.

Lewis, J. A. "A Study of the Effectiveness of Three Methods of Teaching One Segment of Political Science." *Journal of Experimental Education,* 1964, *33,* 73–78.

Lippitt, R., Watson, J., and Westley, B. *The Dynamics of Planned Change.* New York: Harcourt Brace Jovanovich, 1958.

Maguire, L. M. *Observations and Analysis of the Literature on Change.* Philadelphia, Pa.: Research for Better Schools, 1970.

Maloney, J. "Individualized Approach to Developing Independent Learners in the Community College." In R. Sugimoto (Ed.), *Proceedings of the Eighth Annual Conference of the Western College Reading Association.* Anaheim, Calif.: The Western College Reading Association, 1975.

Maxwell, M. *Improving Student Learning Skills: A Comprehensive Guide to Successful Practice and Programs for Increasing the Performance of Underprepared Students.* San Francisco: Jossey-Bass, 1979.

Mayhew, L. B. *How Colleges Change: Approaches to Academic Reform.* Stanford, Calif.: ERIC Clearinghouse on Information Resources, Stanford Center for Research and Development in Teaching, Stanford University, 1976.

National Training Laboratories. *Reading Book: Twentieth Annual Summer Laboratories in Human Relations Training.* Washington, D.C.: National Training Laboratories, 1966.

Roueche, J. E., and Snow, J. J. *Overcoming Learning Problems: A Guide to Developmental Education in College.* San Francisco: Jossey-Bass, 1977.

Spaulding, N. "Five Minicourses in Study Skills." In R. Sugimoto (Ed.), *Proceedings of the Eighth Annual Conference of the Western College Reading Association.* Anaheim, Calif.: The Western College Reading Association, 1975.

Tomlinson, B., and Green, T. "Integrating Reading and Study Skills Adjunct Classes with the Content Areas." In R. Sugimoto (Ed.), *Proceedings of the Ninth Annual Conference of the Western College Reading Association.* Tucson, Ariz.: The Western College Reading Association, 1976.

Tomlinson, B., and Tomlinson, M. "Integrating Reading and Study Skills into College Biology." In W. D. Miller and G. H. McNinch (Eds.), *Reflections and Investigations on Reading: The Twenty-Fifth Yearbook of the National Reading Conference.* Clemson, S.C.: National Reading Conference, 1976.

Whimbey, A. "Teaching Sequential Thought: The Cognitive-Skills Approach." *Phi Delta Kappan,* 1977, *59* (4), 255.

June Dempsey is associate director for Adult Learning Assistance, Diagnostic Learning Center, College of Education, University of Houston Central Campus. She served as director of the Learning Center, division chairperson of Developmental Education, San Joaquin Delta Community College, and president of the Western College Reading Association, and assisted in the establishment of learning center programs in several two- year and four-year institutions.

Barbara Tomlinson is an assistant professor in the Department of Literature and director of the Muir College Writing Program at the University of California, San Diego. As director of the Learning Skills Center, University of California, Irvine, and director of the Learning and Study Skills Center, University of California, Riverside, she developed both centers from their early stages.

Learning support systems are being found to play a significant
role in the retention of students; much potential exists for
helping students at all levels of academic ability to
improve their effectiveness in the learning process
and with it the likelihood of completing their
educational programs.

Learning Centers and Retention

Philip E. Beal

An issue of much concern in higher education today is the problem of attrition and its impact on student enrollment. Numerous research studies have been conducted in the course of the last forty years. Two books with provocative titles were published in 1975, *Preventing Students from Dropping Out* (Astin, 1975) and *Revolving College Doors* (Cope and Hannah, 1975). The bibliography in the latter listed more than 400 works on retention-related research and issues in student retention.

In a paper presented at the annual convention of the American Association for Higher Education, Lenning (1978) discussed what is increasingly a hope for education; namely, maintaining enrollments through better retention. On October 30, 1978, a front-page article in the *Chronicle of Higher Education* identified student retention as the newest and most urgent issue in higher education and described programs to improve retention on three campuses (Middleton, 1978); at these schools, retention increased by as much as 16 percent for students who attended a special orientation session. The chapters of one recent volume (Noel, 1978) focused on programming to improve retention through career planning, admissions management, academic advising, equal opportunity programs, and new educational designs for a new clientele.

Much, if not most, of the research on attrition and retention is focused on factors or indicators that contribute to student attrition and retention at different types of institutions and among students with varying degrees of motivation, academic ability, and educational aspirations. According to Pantages and Creedon (1978), however, most literature reviews on attrition have neglected the substantial number of study recommendations for reducing attrition rates. Little follow-up has been done on the results of such recommendations on the action programs implemented by various institutions with the specific intent of improving student retention.

The lack of information on retention programs should, perhaps, be attributed to the localized nature of institutional efforts, designed as they are to meet the specific needs and conditions of a particular campus. Other institutions that have similar concerns may be unaware of the experience of their neighbors. Further, our review of the literature indicated that no one had attempted to canvass the field systematically to determine what was happening in action programs. Even at professional conferences, where reports of successful endeavors are sometimes given, the audience is limited and the information often cannot be retrieved at a later date. Although the ERIC system is helpful in finding retention-related materials, the focus on action programs per se is still limited.

What Works in Student Retention

A joint project was conceived and implemented in 1978 by the National Center for Higher Education Management Systems (NCHEMS) and the American College Testing Program (ACT), and a national survey entitled "What Works in Student Retention" (WWISR) was conducted. The purpose of the survey was to identify, analyze, and compile information about campus action programs and other efforts aimed at improving student retention in higher education. That is, the project was intended to catalogue retention strategies and procedures found to have improved student retention on college campuses across the country. Findings of the project have broad implications for the role that learning centers can play in institution-wide efforts to improve student retention.

The project design was descriptive in nature, utilizing self-report information from colleges and universities to document what they had done or were doing to improve retention and to evaluate the results. All two- and four-year institutions in the country were included, not only to identify what action programs were under way but also to determine the number of institutions engaged in action programs.

A pilot instrument was reviewed by advisory boards from ACT and NCHEMS and field tested by twenty institutions during Winter 1978-79. Postcards were sent to 2,459 institutions requesting the president to designate an individual to receive and complete a questionnaire.

Returns were received from 1,600 presidents, and questionnaires were sent to the designated individuals. More than 990 completed questionnaires were returned, of which 947 were usable in the study. A total of 1,024 report forms regarding special efforts were received from 387 institutions. Despite the lack of documentation in the literature, the survey found a large number of individual efforts under way on college campuses for the purpose of improving student retention. Many of these programs have been compiled and analyzed by WWISR, and they are discussed in some depth by Beal and Noel (1980).

General Findings

The directors of the study took the perspective that improved student retention is a by-product of institutional improvement related to student development and satisfaction. Retention was not considered a goal likely to be achieved unless an institution deliberately addressed the entire array of concerns involved in "doing a better job of all the things which make up a campus" (Noel, 1978, p. 98). This perspective on retention was endorsed by findings of the study which clearly indicated that improving institutional services can in fact enhance student retention. Many of the services addressed by action programs, such as academic advising, counseling, orientation, and co-curricular activities, were areas that were already receiving some attention on the campus. In other cases, such as learning and academic support programs, early warning systems, and new policies, structures, and curricular developments, the activities had been designed as a result of the new interest in student retention.

In all cases, a focus on retention contributed to the development of new programs and modifications of existing ones, which showed positive results. A total of forty-seven different types of action programs were identified by respondents, and these action programs were combined into fifteen categories. The most frequent type of program, submitted by 24 percent of the schools, involved learning skills and academic support systems—learning centers. These programs were most likely to occur in four-year public institutions, 33 percent of which had such programs, and least likely in four-year private institutions, only 18 percent of which had such programs. Programs involving advising, orientation, and early warning systems—which conceivably could be activities of a learning center—were the next most frequent type of action program.

Approximately forty different target groups were identified by the survey as needing special attention action programs. These target groups were combined into fourteen categories. The target groups to which action programs were most frequently addressed included new students (freshmen and transfers), all students, high-risk students, and an "other" category whose constituents were unique to a given campus. Nine percent of the programs were addressed to students who evidenced low academic performance or who were judged to be potential dropouts. Only 4 percent were addressed to students specifically identified as having various skill deficiencies related to college work, while 3 percent were addressed specifically to women and adults, and 3 percent were aimed at minority students; minority students were occasionally mentioned as recipients of action programs directed at other target groups.

The action activity report forms used in the NCHEMS/ACT survey included rating scales to indicate institutional satisfaction with the program and to estimate the improvement in retention that resulted from the program. In addition, a general impact index and a retention impact index were devised. The general impact index reflected how the campus responded to the action program beyond any consideration of retention improvement. It was apparent from written comments on many forms that the campuses benefited in a variety of ways from new or revised programs. These benefits were often more immediately observable than eventual retention improvements and sometimes led to new outlooks, new programs, and improved campus morale which, it was felt, would enhance retention. Thus, the general impact index illustrated campus attitudes and feelings as much as objective change. As with the retention index, low ratings usually indicated lack of information on results rather than poor results. Three graduate students with experience in content analysis and coding read all the action forms and assigned success indices to the programs.

The impact of action programs on various target groups is presented in Table 1. Only those programs identified on a range of two to five as showing some impact are included. In terms of improved retention, target groups that benefited the most from intervention programs were dropouts, resident students, high-risk students, multiple target groups, and new students. In the case of all target groups, varying degrees of retention improvement did take place. In terms of general campus impact, target groups that showed the greatest benefits were resident students, minority students, others, women and adults, and multiple target groups. However, some degree of positive campus impact occurred with all target groups.

The success index of action programs on retention and general impact is presented in Table 2. Programs emphasizing new policies and structures for retention showed the greatest improvement, followed by new learning/academic support programs, orientation, early-warning systems, and curricular developments. Although programs emphasizing student peer involvement ranked low on retention improvement, they ranked first in general campus impact. In several other cases, including career assistance programs and faculty/staff development, the campus impact appeared to be considerably greater than the retention impact.

Table 1. Retention and General Impact by Target Groups*

| | Retention Index | | General Index | |
	N		N	
Dropouts	9	3.67	16	3.44
Resident students	4	3.50	10	4.40
High-risk	56	3.48	82	3.85
Multiple target groups	13	3.46	31	3.94
New students	102	3.44	182	3.88
Other	46	3.33	82	4.04
All students	48	3.31	112	3.79
Women and adults	8	3.25	24	4.00
Undecided majors and careers	16	3.25	39	3.74
Skill deficiencies	17	3.24	38	3.79
Minority students	11	3.18	20	4.05
Low academic performance	39	3.18	70	3.60
Potential dropouts	42	3.07	71	3.49
Faculty and staff	9	3.00	34	3.74
All	420	3.33	811	3.81

*Range of index 2–5.

Learning Centers and Retention

Although a number of the activities listed in Table 2 could be included in learning centers of the future, of particular interest to this discussion is the role of learning and academic support programs in retention. The comprehensive, in-depth review of student retention theory and research conducted by Lenning, Beal, and Sauer (1980) implies strongly that such programs can have a major positive impact on student retention statistics. Further, it is clear from the data provided to WWISR that learning and academic support programs do have a definite positive impact on retention. Of the 420 programs with an index of two or higher, 115 were learning and academic support programs with a retention index of 3.45. Of the top fifty programs, which showed an improvement in retention of 10 or more percentage points, seventeen were programs dealing with learning and academic support systems. These programs were also found to rate high in terms of general campus impact. Of the 811 report forms that described programs in sufficient detail to allow them to be rated on a general basis, 199 dealt with learning and academic support, with an average index of 3.83.

Learning programs are addressed to a wide variety of target populations. Figure 1 shows the various target groups for learning programs and the general and retention impact which these programs had. The lower circle indicates that 115 programs were rated for their impact on retention, using an index of two to five; the average index for these 115 programs was 3.45. Twelve were addressed to new students, with a retention index of 3.42; thirty-seven programs to high-risk students,

Table 2. Retention and General Impact by Action Programs*

	Retention Index N		General Index N	
New policies, structures	11	3.64	26	3.92
Learning, academic support	115	3.45	199	3.83
Orientation	68	3.44	115	3.91
Early-warning systems	45	3.38	97	3.56
Curricular developments	6	3.33	13	3.92
Multiple action programs	14	3.29	25	4.04
Advising	61	3.26	115	3.78
Career assistance	23	3.26	49	4.00
Counseling	18	3.22	30	3.80
Peer programs	9	3.22	31	4.13
Faculty/staff development	10	3.20	25	4.00
Other	12	3.00	32	3.88
Dropout studies	9	3.22	12	3.33
Co-curricular activities	4	2.75	20	3.70
Exit interviews	15	2.67	22	3.23
All	420	3.33	811	3.81

*Range of index 2–5.

with a retention impact of 3.57, and so forth. An index of two to five was used to rate the general impact of 199 programs; here the average index was 3.83. Again, these programs were directed to a variety of target groups.

The most common learning and academic support program described in this survey incorporated a full range of services, including personal tutoring, credit or noncredit group or class experiences in a wide assortment of learning skills, group help or lab sessions related to particular courses or disciplines, behavior or learning contracts, and career-related learning services, in various combinations. In some cases, the program was known as a learning center. The majority of these programs were addressed to low-performance and high-risk students, although several other target groups were also identified. The other programs identified were more narrow in scope, involving only one or two forms of learning assistance, though the target groups were similar to those of the full-range programs.

In the following section, examples of various learning and academic support programs are listed. The material is taken from the original report form supplied by the institution or from follow-up correspondence. The programs listed include full-range programs, tutoring, credit courses for learning skills, and noncredit classes and lab sessions. In each case, the nature of the program, the institution, the target group, the general impact of the program, and the retention impact are identified.

Figure 1. General Impact Index*

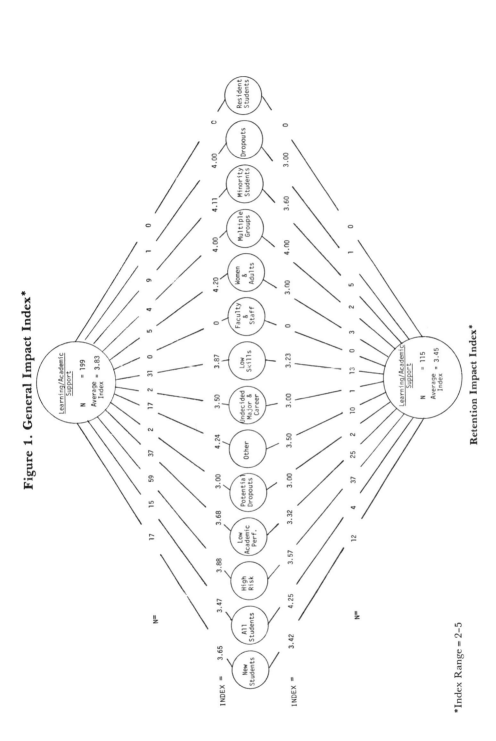

Retention Impact Index*

*Index Range = 2–5

Full-Range Programs. 1. *Program*—Two-day workshop prior to fall semester, weekly group meetings with peer advisers during the first nine weeks of semester focused on help with immediate concerns, academic adjustment, and study skills.

- *School*—University of Northern Iowa, Cedar Falls.
- *Target Group*—Freshmen with low composite ACT scores or lower half of high school graduation class.
- *Impact*—Of 239 students invited to participate, 115 did so. Follow-up evaluation indicated that the program had helped the students to understand academic requirements, improve study skills, understand instructor's teaching methods, improve testing techniques, adjust to the university, and, improve self-image.
- *Retention*—7.8 percent of the participants did not return for the second semester, compared to 18 percent of the noninvited nonparticipants and 17.7 percent of the invited nonparticipants. Of 76 pairs matching participants with noninvited nonparticipants, participants achieved a GPA of 1.998, compared to 1.729 for nonparticipants (a .01 level of significance).

2. *Program*—An individual needs program for first-semester students providing comprehensive, supportive service involving intensive academic and vocational counseling, tutoring, block programming, performance monitoring, study skills training, and personal attention to bureaucratic problems.

- *School*—Loop College, Chicago, Illinois.
- *Target Group*—High-risk first-semester freshmen, including both recent high school graduates and older returning students.
- *Impact*—The number of students on academic probation was reduced. Over 90 percent of participants indicated greater confidence in meeting the challenges of college work after time in the program. Of the 129 fall semester students who received intensive career counseling, all made declarations of majors and chose specific programs. An informal group of faculty interested in teaching developmental level courses was formed to work with the program director to establish developmental curriculums each semester. Learning center resources were expanded to include self-instructional programs and delivery systems for skills rebuilding. Tutors were permanently staffed, using renewable project money.
- *Retention*—Retention improved to 89 percent, compared to a school-wide average of 48 percent. No figures on high-risk per se were available for previous years.

3. *Program*—Academic assistance, including free minicourses, reading lab, group and individual personal counseling, and student orientation.

- *School*—Pan American University, Edinburgh, Texas.
- *Target group*—Freshmen and sophomores who experience difficulty.
- *Impact*—Many faculty began to refer students to supportive services. Departmental curriculums were modified to include lab and individualized course work. General morale for assisting academically disadvantaged students has increased.
- *Retention*—After two years of college, retention of users of these services was 18.4 percent greater than retention of nonusers matched by ACT scores, classification, and ethnicity,

4. *Program*—A study skills program, providing individualized help and workshops.

- *School*—Whittier College, Whittier, California.
- *Targeted Group*—Freshmen on academic warning or probation.
- *Impact*—Improved quality of courses, improved tuition income, improved student self-image.
- *Retention*—A 90 percent retention rate for those who completed the program, against approximately 70 percent for a control group.

5. *Program*—A variety of remedial courses in reading, math, and English fundamentals, two learning skills centers for math and writing, special preadmission testing and mandated personal interviews.

- *School*—Pierce Junior College, Philadelphia, Pennsylvania.
- *Target Group*—All entering first-time freshmen.
- *Impact*—Students with academic deficiencies are diagnosed, and a reduced academic load, appropriate remedial courses or both are prescribed. Students show less resistance to remedial courses. Academic dismissals reduced by 25 to 30 percent.
- *Retention*—Over two years, the retention rate increased from 70 percent to 79 percent.

6. *Program*—Student learning center providing supplemental class instruction utilizing a unique model of teaching basic skills through content areas; not a drop-in center. Staff members were assigned to courses likely to be high-risk for students.

- *School*—University of Missouri, Kansas City, Missouri.
- *Target Group*—Health sciences students (especially minority and disadvantaged) and students in entry-level arts and sciences courses.
- *Impact*—Faculty appear more aware of need for academic support services. Training in learning skills has been provided to

graduate teaching assistants. Department and school requests for learning center programs have increased significantly. Faculty are increasingly disposed to suggest that students utilize the learning center.

- *Retention*—Minority attrition in health sciences has all but ceased. Overall medical student attrition has dropped from 16 to 2 percent. Minority attrition has dropped 100 percent in pharmacy. Undergraduate attrition in target arts and sciences courses has declined by 20 to 50 percent.

7. *Program*—A learning center providing comprehensive academic support services, including orientation, peer tutoring, minicourses, and a learning lab.

- *School*—West Liberty State College, West Liberty, West Virginia.
- *Target Group*—Total student body.
- *Impact*—Faculty awareness of the retention issue and student learning needs has increased. Learning center serves as clearinghouse for student requests, provides students with skills, instruction, and learning options. After four years, the learning center is an established program on campus, with staff, budget, academic credit, and physical facility.
- *Retention*—First semester attrition rate for freshmen who sought learning center services was 11.4 percent, compared with 17.6 percent for total freshmen. The overall college attrition rate decreased by 4 percent.

Tutoring. Many programs emphasized counseling or tutoring for students exhibiting a need or interest in special assistance.

1. *Program*—As a part of the orientation program, all freshmen in the fourth week of classes complete a questionnaire designed to identify academic and personal problems. Counseling and tutoring are provided for students in need of such services.

- *School*—Mount Mary College, Milwaukee, Wisconsin.
- *Target Group*—All new freshmen.
- *Impact*—The freshmen orientation program took on added dimensions. First-hand data made it possible to channel tutoring services more effectively. The need for additional counseling personnel became apparent.
- *Retention*—During the past two years, there has been a decided drop in freshmen withdrawals. Lack of statistically reliable data precludes a definitive statement on success, the number of withdrawals before the end of first semester was 20 percent lower than levels in previous years.

2. *Program*—Pretesting at three levels of mathematics: beginning, precalculus, and calculus, follow-up counseling for student place-

ment proctors providing individual attention in tutorial sections; mini-course assistance and instant feedback on test results.

- *School*—Lamar University, Beaumont, Texas.
- *Target Group*—Entering freshmen and students enrolling in their first mathematics course.
- *Impact*—The program increases basic knowledge and the probability of success in degree-required mathematics courses and underlines the university's commitment to its open enrollment policy.
- *Retention*—In the last three years, the attrition rate in the main line course has dropped at least 10 percent.

3. *Program*—Special tutorial services.

- *School*—Longview Community College, Lee's Summit, Missouri.
- *Target Group*—General student body.
- *Impact*—The academic achievement level, class withdrawal rate, and attrition rate of participants improved, compared with the rest of the student body. The program increased faculty sensitivity and awareness of the learning needs of students who differ in age, educational background, and learning styles.
- *Retention*—The term-to-term retention rate for participants was more than 20 percent higher than for students in general.

4. *Program*—Counselor working with students during a probationary period.

- *School*—Auburn University, Montgomery, Alabama.
- *Target Group*—Special students, probationary admissions.
- *Impact*—Students demonstrate a more positive attitude. Enrollment has increased. Prospective students see a greater chance for success.
- *Retention*—Seventy-five percent qualify to continue in attendance as regular students, compared to 50 percent prior to special counseling.

5. *Program*—Individual academic tutoring in twenty-two department subject areas.

- *School*—Weaver State College, Ogden, Utah.
- *Target Group*—Students of all ability levels needing help in their academic work.
- *Impact*—Participation in the tutoring program has increased from 1,771 students in 1974–75 to 6,480 students in 1977–78.
- *Retention*—No numerical impact data were available.

6. *Program*—Free campus-wide tutoring program, which includes upperclass tutors recommended by departments, a tutoring center, materials for tutoring, and campus funds allotted to paid tutors and evaluation procedures.

- *School* — Grand Valley State Colleges, Allendale, Michigan.
- *Target Group* — Any currently enrolled student.
- *Impact* — Faculty members refer students for the free tutoring. The faculty role in nominating tutors has increased. Students themselves are seeking out the free unlimited tutoring program.
- *Retention* — The potential effectiveness of this program is untested thus far.

7. *Program* — A tutoring service in the areas of mathematics, writing, and reading skills, which stresses basic skills in the arenas of vocabulary, outlining, punctuation, sentence structure, research papers, comprehension, reading speed, and mathematical concepts.

- *School* — Univesota of Minnesota, Morris, Minnesota.
- *Target Group* — Students with a need for academic assistance. (About 9 percent were minority students.)
- *Impact* — Three tutors worked with fifty-three students, with an average of ten visits per student. Many participating students completed course work with passing grades. Tutors encourage students to seek help from their instructors, which has helped instructors to become more aware of special learning difficulties.
- *Retention* — Retention of minority students has increased. More students have used the program as they became aware of its benefits.

Credit Courses for Learning Skills. A large number of programs included group sessions for the teaching of learning skills. In many cases, these involved credit courses taught by faculty, learning skills specialists, or peer counselors.

1. *Program* — Education 1201, "Improvement of Learning Skills," two credit hours, pass/no pass: an elective course taught by peer counselors enrolled in Education 2301, "Peer Advisor-Counselor Training," (three credit hours). The peer counselors received specific skills training from the director of retention.

- *School* — Lamar University, Beaumont, Texas.
- *Target Group* — All students, including very bright able learners and students with potential academic problems.
- *Impact* — Since its introduction, 724 students have successfully completed the course. Due to positive student attitudes and research results, faculty members are increasingly recommending the course to marginal students and offering to assist peer counselors in appropriate ways. Students cited improvement in study habits and attitudes toward learning as major reasons for improved GPAs and positive feelings toward the university and education.

- *Retention* — Of students with ACT scores of 15 or below or composite SAT scores of 700 or below, 59.1 percent were still enrolled four semesters later, compared with expected retention of less than 30 percent. Average pre-post scores on a survey of study habits and attitudes increased by 40 percent.

2. *Program* — Special sections for "College Algebra."
   - *School* — University of Pittsburgh, Pittsburgh, Pennsylvania.
   - *Target Group* — Students with insufficient math preparation.
   - *Impact* — Integration of math learning skills with academic department. Small classes enhance the teaching and learning environment. Target number of students was able to enter higher level math courses, with better performance in math-related courses.
   - *Retention* — Failure rate decreased from 32 percent to 8 percent.

3. *Program* — Required lab for developmental English and reading courses, one credit hour.
   - School — Gulf Coast Community College, Panama City, Florida.
   - *Target Group* — Students needing remediation in basic skills in math, reading, and English.
   - *Impact* — Positive impact on programs and enrollment data.
   - *Retention* — Nearly 30 percent improvement in retention rate.

4. *Program* — Learning center program (two credits) involving reading for increased speed and comprehension, study skills, and tutorials.
   - *School* — Baldwin Wallace College, Berea, Ohio.
   - *Target Group* — High-risk students identified upon admission.
   - *Impact* — Former learning center students have been active as leaders on campus. Two former learning center students have been recent senior class presidents.
   - *Retention* — Eighty-three percent in 1976, 91 percent in 1977. In 1978–79, the mean GPA of students referred to program was 1.019; after one quarter of learning center assistance, the mean GPA was 2.343.

Noncredit Courses and Sessions. Noncredit courses or sessions, including lab sessions or special help sessions, were often a part of student learning support systems.

1. *Program* — Specialists in development of learning skills teach extra support sessions of basic required lab courses.
   - *School* — Husson College, Bangor, Maine.
   - *Target Group* — Educational or culturally disadvantaged and physically handicapped students.
   - *Impact* — Faculty frustration at not having enough time to devote to the full range of student competencies in a class has

decreased. The college is more aware that some semingly hopeless students can succeed if basic support services are provided. Fewer scheduling adjustments, particularly for freshmen, were noticed.

- *Retention* — Course failures were reduced by 40 percent.

2. *Program* — Developmental studies courses in reading, writing, and math.

- *School* — Utica College, Utica, New York.
- *Target Group* — Borderline admissions from incoming freshmen classes.
- *Impact* — Better preparation for college-level courses and less opportunity for failure.
- *Retention* — Sixty-three percent retention of participating students over a one-year period.

3. *Program* — Accounting lab offering a regularly scheduled walk-in clinic and individualized tutoring on an appointment basis.

- *School* — Towson State University, Towson, Maryland.
- *Target Group* — Students enrolled in accounting courses at all levels.
- *Impact* — As a referral service for instructors and a valuable resource for students, the lab reduces the number of students repeating courses and thereby the need for extra sections of lower-level accounting courses.
- *Retention* — Retention of students in accounting courses has improved.

Conclusions

Many of the programs and services briefly described above will not be new to the reader. What the reader may not realize is the potential for a direct relationship between learning centers and retention. College administrators and faculty may not at first recognize how learning assistance programs can also improve academic satisfaction. Although these programs have traditionally focused on remedial components, the most significant and most exciting efforts appear to be directed at all students who want to improve their learning skills, whatever their level of academic performance.

From the examples submitted to WWISR, it appears that institutional renewal and vitality are frequent by-products of new efforts to establish learning and academic support services. When faculty members, administrators, student services personnel, and students collaborate in efforts to increase the effectiveness of learning and its relevance to student goals, the resultant enthusiasm may itself be a factor in the increased retention. Institutions that provide lively learning experiences for students, involve students in the learning process, and offer personalized opportunities for interactions with faculty and other students are likely to find attractive retention rates as a by-product. Improved retention is difficult to achieve as a goal in itself. One affect of the development of learning and academic support services is that students can better identify their own goals, skills, and directions and relate them to what the college or university has to offer. Well-designed learning centers that involve faculty, students, and administrators in their conceptualization and operation can play a crucial role in student retention.

References

Astin, A. W. *Preventing Students from Dropping Out.* San Francisco: Jossey-Bass, 1975.

Beal, P. E., and Noel, L. *What Works in Student Retention?* Iowa City, Iowa: American College Testing Program, 1980.

Cope, R. G., and Hannah, W. *Revolving College Doors.* New York: Wiley, 1975.

Lenning, O. T. "An Optimistic Alternative: Keeping Enrollment Up." Paper presented at annual convention of the American Association for Higher Educaion, Chicago, March 1978.

Lenning, O. T., Beal, P. E., and Sauer, K. *Attrition and Retention: Evidence for Action and Research.* Boulder, Colo.: National Center for Higher Education Management Systems, in press.

Middleton, I. "With Freshmen Scarcer, Emphasis Shifts to Keeping Present Students." *The Chronicle of Higher Education,* October, 30, 1978, p. 1.

Noel, L. "First Steps in Starting a Campus Retention Program." In L. Noel (Ed.), *New Directions for Student Services: Reducing the Dropout Rate,* no. 3. San Francisco: Jossey-Bass, 1978.

Pantages, T. J., and Creedon, C. F. "Studies of College Attrition." *Review of Educational Research,* 1978, *48,* 49-101.

Philip E. Beal, dean of students at Saginaw Valley State College, has experience in university administration, graduate teaching, and research. As a visiting scholar at the National Center for Higher Education Management Systems (1978–79) he initiated and codirected a national study on "What Works in Student Retention" (WWISR). He has presented numerous seminars on student retention as well as conference presentations at both the American Association for Higher Education and the American Council of Education. He also served on the National Executive Committee of NAPSA and held other offices on a regional basis.

Successful evaluations consider politics and personalities as well as judgments when assessing the need for a learning center, determining strategies for improving learning center operations, and assessing total institutional impact.

Evaluating Learning Centers

Robert R. Brown

As indicated elsewhere in this volume and in Maxwell (1979), the establishment of learning centers on American campuses took place within a national and local campus political context. Political support and external funding were sufficient to launch new programs and often to sustain them. The student protest movement of the nineteen sixties and the increased access to higher education brought about by federal financial aid programs and open admissions policies resulted in special programming to meet the diverse learning needs of new students. There are reported to be 1,848 learning center components in 1,433 colleges and universities (Sullivan, 1978).

Today, learning centers are competing with other programs for the same shrinking dollar. The political honeymoon for learning centers is over. They have to provide evidence of worth and show whether they can do more for less. Economic conditions interact with politics, and in the nineteen eighties, administrators are concentrating not on program expansion but on resource reallocation. In this political and economic climate, programs which are not seen as inherently part of the academic enterprise must demonstrate their worth with evaluative data.

This chapter proposes a definition of evaluation and important distinctions in terminology and kinds of evaluation. A three-phase scheme for conducting an evaluation examines different evaluation approaches and key issues and questions. By providing a framework for decisions on important evaluation questions and sources for specific models and approaches, this chapter should assist those who plan or commission an evaluation of learning centers.

Evaluation Defined

Evaluation is a natural activity, as much a part of everyday life as is breathing. It involves judgments of worth as defined by social utility (Worthen and Sanders, 1973). These judgments lead to decisions and actions. These considerations also apply to formal evaluation. "To evaluate is to make judgments about the worth of a program or elements of a program. The worth of a program is ultimately determined by its impact on society as well as on its participants and those within the immediate context. Criteria for determination of worth can include the extent of the program's impact, the number of persons affected, cost-benefit analysis, and other program and person dimensions. Worth can be determined relative to the program's goals, in comparison to other programs, or to other standards. The evaluative judgments lead to decisions which have a direct impact on whether the program is continued, expanded, reduced in scope, or otherwise changed. The evaluative judgment can be formal and explicit, based on an intentional and extensive data collection process, and include a publicly announced decision. Because evaluation is a natural human activity, it can also be informal, based on whatever information is available at the moment, and quite private" (Brown, 1978, p. 14).

This definition suggests that evaluation can be simple or quite complex. For this reason, it is important to understand differences in the kinds and purposes of evaluation. Among these are the differences between research and evaluation, formative and summative evaluation, external and internal evaluation, and program and personnel evaluation.

Research Versus Evaluation. The purpose of scientific research is to develop theory, reach conclusions about cause and effect relationships, and make generalizations that are applicable to other situations and settings (Kerlinger, 1973). A person conducting scientific research on learning centers would develop theories about how students learn, determine precisely what functions of learning centers maximize learning, and discover whether general principles apply to students in a variety of settings. These are worthy goals, but they necessitate strict control over many extraneous variables which usually can be achieved only in a highly controlled laboratory environment. These conditions are seldom possible in a learning center setting.

In contrast, evaluation focuses on questions of worth and the decisions that must be made about a center. The evaluator recognizes that cost-effectiveness, staff and student morale, and faculty attitudes play an important part in assessing the effectiveness of a center. An evaluator may wish to use an experimental research design as part of an evaluation design, but seldom will the research design be comprehensive enough to suffice by itself (Patton, 1978).

Formative Versus Summative Evaluation. Formative evaluation assists the center during its development (Scriven, 1967). It provides feedback to program developers so changes can be made to improve the center. The evaluator serves as a troubleshooter, getting information to the staff as quickly as possible. Very often, formative evaluation is conducted by a staff member, perhaps as a participant observer, or by a team. Informal reports are made primarily to center staff.

In contrast, summative evaluation is intended to provide information to an external person, often a funder, consumer, or decision maker, that influences continuation or level of funding. Usually, it is conducted by an unbiased third person at a strategic terminal point. A formal report is made available to persons external to the center staff.

Formative evaluation can be compared to tests conducted along an auto assembly line when it is possible to make corrections, whereas a summative evaluation would be conducted on the final product by a consumer magazine, safety inspectors, or buyers themselves. In several ways, a formative evaluation has more utility, because it is conducted by a staff member familiar with the inner workings of the center and committed to its success. A summative evaluation is usually conducted by an outsider who knows less about the program and whose intent is to facilitate judgments rather than improve the center.

External and Formal Versus Internal and Informal Evaluation. The distinctions between these kinds of evaluation are implicit in the discussion of formative and summative evaluation. Formative is usually synonymous with internal and informal, summative with external and formal. There may be exceptions. For example, learning center staff may believe that they are too personally involved to allow students to be as candid with them as with an objective outsider, and as a result they may want to commission an external person to interview students and observe center operations. How formal the evaluation is depends on the needs of the center and the kind of report that will be made and to whom.

Program Versus Personnel Evaluation. In some instances, personnel evaluation is a component of program evaluation. The scheme provided here recognizes that people are inherently part of a program. However, the focus of program evaluation is on judging the program, not people. The chances of an evaluation being useful are greater, especially for formative evaluation, if staff are not fearful that the evaluation information will be used against them. It is essential for these two types of evaluation to remain distinct. If they are conducted at the same time, they should be performed by different persons. Program evaluation should facilitate mutual problem solving rather than self-protection.

The learning center director who keeps these distinctions clear should be able to clarify the purpose of the evaluation, and as the purpose becomes clearer, the choice of relevant evaluation strategies will become easier.

Evaluation Scheme for Learning Centers

This evaluation scheme provides a framework for designing and conducting an evaluation of a learning center; it takes the developmental phase of the center into account. Three phases are considered: establishment, installation and improvement, and assessing impact. The audience, relevant questions, and strategies vary, depending upon the phase. The questions asked during the establishment phase must be re-examined continually, however, because for higher education the passage of time results in changing student enrollment patterns, new faculty members with different perspectives, and new curriculums with different options and requirements. Those who plan to start a learning center will want to work systematically through all phases, while those evaluating a center which has been in existence for several years will also find many of the questions and procedures described in Phases I and II equally necessary.

Phase I: Establishment. The impetus for a new learning center on campus may originate with a staff or faculty member who hears about the success of such a center on a comparable campus, or an administrator may bring the idea to campus from his or her work at another institution. In some states, legislators have been instrumental in establishing policies that resulted in the establishment of a learning center (McEwen, 1979). There are three evaluative questions in this phase: Is there a need for a learning center? Is a learning center feasible? Is the climate receptive? Evaluation activities during Phase I focus on obtaining information needed to answer these questions.

Is There a Need for a Learning Center? As with many other evaluation questions, there is no formula that provides a straightforward answer to questions of need. Need is arbitrary, sometimes relative, and always a matter of judgment. Need must first be distinguished from want (Lenning and McAleenan, 1979). Students may indicate they would like to have tutoring in mathematics, but this does not necessarily mean that they "need" it. A mathematics professor may believe that students need tutoring, even though many students may not want it.

A needs analysis should provide information specific enough to make decisions about the kind and amount of services that a learning center will provide. In what subject areas are tutorial services needed? Are preparatory courses in reading, writing, mathematics, and other basic skills needed? Are unique counseling services needed? Should there be a study skills course? Should certain students be required to participate? These are examples of questions that must be answered.

A good needs analysis also assesses the unique needs of different students. Do the needs of students in science courses differ from the needs of students in business? Do ethnic minority students have more or less need for counseling services? What kind of needs do mature adults have for counseling, study skills, and tutorial assistance? Discovering the unique needs of different students makes it possible to earmark services and establish priorities.

The information necessary to develop a needs statement comes from a variety of sources, including national publications, existing local records, and current and former students and faculty. The types of information that are most helpful include admission test results, high school performance information, and attrition rates. An expectancy table will indicate the likelihood with which students with varying scores and achievement records will survive to complete their academic programs. Such a table will undoubtedly indicate that completion rates increase as admission scores and past performance indicators increase. However, when this statistical information is combined with a profile of those who complete the program, it will be seen that a sizable percentage of the students in the lowest quartile also succeed. This suggests that if some students with poor academic indicators can succeed, so can others. Perhaps success is a question of the services that are available.

Attrition data alone may be sufficient to convince certain audiences of the need for a learning center, especially if the potential for increased retention is translated into tuition dollars. Retention promises to be an increasing concern in higher education, and it may not take a large increase in retention that can be attributed to a learning center to make the center cost-effective.

Long, massive surveys of student and faculty attitudes should be avoided. Consider these alternatives: Check the literature for relevant recent information from comparable institutions; perhaps an institution of similar size and makeup recently initiated a student learning center and conducted a needs analysis with results that could be applied to your institution. If necessary, replicate one of the studies you discovered with a smaller sample. Find out what relevant information is available from local attrition studies that employed exit interviews. Also use expert opinion from credible campus sources. Whichever strategy is employed, testimonials from current and former students who were helped by services already available or who indicate that they would have utilized such a service if it had been available are always useful. Testimonials personalize tables and other numerical data and potentially have a dramatic impact on decision makers.

Is a Learning Center Feasible? Feasibility plays an important role in determining whether a learning center will be started and the form that it will take if it is established. Feasibility is affected by the concept of what constitutes a learning center (Maxwell, 1979). Does it mean expanding services available in an existing agency, such as a counseling center? Does it mean coordinating effort through establishment of an information resource center? Or does it mean coalescing a variety of resources into one unit? Choosing among these alternatives requires a comprehensive awareness of current services.

Several lists and analysis are necessary. One list should include all agencies offering related services; this information can be obtained from available program descriptions or through interviews and questionnaires. Another list should include campus personnel who have training, expertise, and interest that match those needed for a learning center. Finally, one list should identify the space and equipment available, so that additional needs in these areas can be assessed.

Ultimately, costs must be considered, both start-up and maintenance. The information on available resources provides a clue as to the amount of additional funding that is required or whether reallocation of existing resources will suffice. The political and economic climate will often determine how much external funding can be obtained. If a favorable balance between costs and increased tuition revenue can be projected, the probability of funding is greater.

Is the Climate Receptive? It is possible for an administrator to have sufficient political clout to establish a learning center even if it means realigning staff responsibilities. However, whether the center will function properly is going to depend upon those who refer students and staff to the center. Receptivity is influenced by the institution's orientation to students with special needs. Is there a "sink or swim" philosophy among administrators and faculty? Are there such options as bankruptcy semesters to make it possible for students to wipe out a disastrous semester? What is the history of remedial courses or special orientation programs? Who has supported such efforts? Who has opposed such programs? Ultimately, most programs survive or die through faculty support or lack of it. Will faculty support a center? Do faculty recognize the need? Will faculty refer students to the center? Will faculty participate in planning the center? Can center programs or courses be made available for academic credit?

The concerns of staff and agency heads who currently offer related services are also critical. How do these agencies feel about transferring a function, if that is necessary? How do staff feel about working somewhere else, if staff realignment is necessary? Staff members will deliver the services, and the quality of the program rests with them and thier support.

It is not easy to determine receptivity. Vocal opposition is obvious enough, but passive aggressive reactions are difficult to uncover. One strategy is to get potential antagonists involved in planning the evaluation (Walberg, 1973). If faculty or staff are surveyed as part of a needs assessment, behavioral as well as attitudinal items should be included. Ask whether they would like to be involved in designing, implementing, or maintaining the center as well as whether they think the concept is a good idea.

These three questions make it apparent that thinking about evaluation needs to begin early. Important persons make judgments about the worth of a learning center even before it has been established. Failure to take this into account can affect the likelihood that the center will get started and its viability in the future if it does.

Phase II: Installation and Improvement. The primary purpose of evaluation at this stage is to assist staff in improving center programs and services. Generally, this evaluation is formative and informal. As such, the primary audience is internal—director and staff. However, periodic updating on student use and programs can also interest external audiences, especially if expansion of services is proposed.

It is important to have information available to improve the center's operation. Much needed information can be obtained through records, short questionnaires, and interviews. As well as providing data for longitudinal studies, the monitoring process sends out a signal the minute that something goes awry.

There are three basic questions that must be answered during this phase: Who uses the services and why? Are the intended services, events, and interactions occurring? What functions of the learning center can be improved?

Who Uses the Services and Why? Staff can get caught up in a numbers game. That is, the more students they work with, the better they view the services. It is just as important, however, that the right students are using the services. Is the center being utilized by the students for whom it was designed? It is not unusual to offer a program to improve reading speed and comprehension, for example, and discover that those enrolled in it already read 800 words per minute with 95 percent comprehension, while those who read 180 words per minute with 65 percent comprehension are not in the program because they are trying to keep up with their course reading assisgnments. This is not to suggest that fast readers should be excluded from using center services, but rather to indicate it would be misleading to use this as supporting evidence for a center developed on the premise it would assist students in the lowest quartile.

Demographic information should be collected from students who use center services. Data may be collected anonymously, but they should always include information on sex, major, ethnic background, GPA, and ability level, whether self-reported or obtained from existing records. This information should be summarized and compared both with intended program clientele and with the general college profile. A representative sample of current users should be asked why they use the services and how they heard about them. Additional comparisons between students who follow through on services and those who do not are also helpful.

Are the Intended Services Being Provided? One reason why many programs fail is that they do not provide the services promised. Expected events do not occur. Many times the breakdowns are due to lack of communication. A mathematics professor may forget to mention to one or two classes that tutoring services are available. Maybe students think they have to be in a special group to be eligible. Or hostility can be the cause. A chemistry professor may undercut the value of the tutoring services because of an unfortunate incident with one tutor, who is no longer on campus.

There are other ways in which programs can break down. An instructor of a study skills class may believe that most academic problems are motivational and decide to spend a disproportionate amount of time in group counseling. The instructor is well intentioned, and students may benefit significantly, but a few may also fail, because they lack some basic study skills.

Having staff keep logs or diaries and having regularly scheduled staff meetings that provide opportunities to share problems are constructive ways of monitoring program implementation. There is no substitute for occasional visits or observations.

How Can the Program Be Improved? Ideas for program improvement will be generated by activities required to determine who uses the services. It is possible to determine whether dissemination of information about the program or student recruitment procedures need to be revised. Other activities that can be helpful include examining outcome data for specific center components, collecting student opinion on what works and what needs to be improved, and obtaining staff input on what needs to be changed.

Evaluating Individual Components. The relative quality of various center components may differ. It is important to assess the effectiveness of each component and how it contributes to the whole. Should more resources and time be devoted to study skills and time management or to tutoring in specific subjects? Each person can be made responsible for evaluating his or her own unit, but relationships among the components can best be examined by an individual from outside the center or by a team of center staff. Depending on the size of learning center staff, the questions regarding individual components are analogous to formative evaluation, whereas questions relating to the reallocation of resources among several components are comparable to summative evaluation. Process and task analysis evaluation approaches are particularly relevant for program monitoring (Provus, 1971).

Obtaining Student Opinion. The reactions of students can be obtained through interviews, questionnaires, or both, administered during or after their involvement in center activities. Several alternatives or supplements to the traditional mailed questionnaire should be considered. Some students can be asked to maintain logs in which they record events, reactions, and ideas as they participated; such logs are a useful mechanism for portraying center activities as well as for gaining insights into program needs. Interviewing students individually or collectively can be another useful technique. An informal or formal student advisory panel can involve students in shaping the evaluation plan. The main questions that need to be asked of students include these: How do they like the program? What are they getting out of the program? What suggestions do they have for improvement? Would they recommend the services to others?

Obtaining Staff Input. Staff should be encouraged to view evaluation as ongoing and useful. It should be seen not as an event, but as a process. However, if this view is to prevail, there must be frequent opportunities for staff input, and there must be follow-up on staff suggestions. Depending upon the size of staff, evaluation should be a regular topic at staff meetings, and an atmosphere respective to evaluative reactions should be maintained. Most of this information can be obtained informally. Particularly sensitive issues may warrant anonymous questionnaires or a suggestion box as data sources.

Phase II evaluation activities should not end when it becomes necessary to conduct the kind of summative evaluation that comes in Phase III. Some Phase II activities can be integrated with Phase III activities and others can be streamlined, but process evaluation should continue.

Phase III: Assessing Impact. The time will come when a new administrator or board member questions the need or value of the learning center. A budget crunch may force re-examination of a number of programs. This can affect the very existence of the center or determine whether the scope of the center will be expanded or limited. Evaluation of impact is generally external, formal, and summative.

In Phase III, there are three key evaluation questions: What are the criteria for assessing the worth of a learning center? What evaluation design should be utilized? How should the information be reported?

What Are the Criteria for Assessing Worth? There are two guidelines for determining specific criteria to use in assessing worth: Collect information related to criteria deemed important by the intended evaluation audience, and attend to as many criteria as possible. It is important to determine the criteria that decision makers will use to make judgments about the center. For example, it does little good to spend time surveying student and faculty opinion when the criterion for success is exclusively the GPA of student participants. It is helpful, but not always possible, to determine the criteria by which the center will be judged prior to its establishment. However, it is essential that criteria be known before the evaluation is completed and results are reported.

It may be necessary to educate the evaluation audience on appropriate and possible criteria. Compile data on as many relevant variables as possible. Consider collecting information on possible side effects, negative as well as positive. Just as the learning center was not conceived in a vacuum, neither does it exist in one. Its impact should be most direct on students, but other direct and indirect impacts are possible. Criteria for a summative evaluation of a learning center should include the impact that the center has had on students, faculty, and the institution.

STUDENT CHANGE. The primary concern will be on the center's direct effects on student achievement and retention. This information should be recorded and made available by semester. It is more relevant to analyze the math grades of students who have been tutored in math than it is to use their total GPA. Information on retention will also be of prime interest. Identify the current status of students who have utilized the learning center. Determine how many are still at the institution or have completed their program. The length of time it took to complete the program may also be of interest.

While achievement and retention are ultimate goals, evaluation of a learning center should also consider what are sometimes referred to as enabling objectives, prerequisite skills necessary to achieve a terminal goal, whether completion of the whole program or a passing grade in a given course. Many learning center programs are designed to improve such enabling skills as study skills, reading speed and comprehension, writing skills, math skills, career development knowledge, and time management skills. Evaluation of a learning center should include assessment of student progress in acquiring fundamental skills that enable them to achieve success in courses and academic programs.

Data on student use of the learning center are also helpful. Descriptions of the number and kinds of students who utilize its services make it possible to determine whether the services are utilized by the intended clientele. Such information is important during the installation and improvement phase, but it also provides an external decision maker with a picture of center activities and clientele.

Finally, student attitudes should not be overlooked. How do student users and non-users feel about the center? Do students feel that the center provides useful services? Do users attribute a share of their success to participation in center activities? Would they recommend the service to other students? Do students who use the center have more positive attitudes towards the institution itself? Do they feel that the faculty and the institution provide enough personal attention? Are they likely to recommend the institution to other students because of the learning center.?

These measures of student change include long-range changes (GPA and retention), short-term changes (study skills, specific skill improvements), and behavioral (usage) and attitudinal (satisfaction) changes. While the long-range behavioral changes are the most important goal, a comprehensive evaluation will also examine short-term and attitudinal changes. Lenning (1976) discusses such outcomes at some length.

FACULTY CHANGE. Faculty attitudes and behaviors are critical, for they affect the extent to which a learning center will be utilized and they may even determine its continued existence. This has implications for programming as well as for evaluation. Faculty perceptions of the utility of the learning center concept and the effectiveness and value of particular services that it offers should be assessed. The best evidence is documentation of faculty referrals and usage, as these behavioral indices reflect their attitudes. The existence of a learning center and interaction with its staff can also affect faculty perceptions of how students learn, which in turn may cause them to reorganize course content and change instructional strategies.

INSTITUTIONAL CHANGE. If the learning center has an active and effective outreach program, curriculum changes may occur. Prerequisites for courses may be added or dropped, new courses may be expanded or deleted. Recruitment and admissions policies and practices may also be affected. Documented success of a learning center will interest student recruiters.

Even more significantly, the attitude of the institution towards instruction and students may be influenced by the activities of center staff. Staff who recognize their political origins and sustenance should acknowledge the value of working directly with administrators and faculty as well as with students. Evidence of impact on institutional philosophies may be difficult to obtain, but it still should be sought.

What Evaluation Models Should Be Utilized? The appropriateness of a particular evaluation model for a summative evaluation depends upon the specific purpose and context of the evaluation. Three broad categories serve to include most of the possibilities: cause and effect models, descriptive models, and issue-resolving models.

CAUSE AND EFFECT MODELS. This is a research approach, which, in view of the distinction made earlier between research and evaluation, may not be appropriate. However, because it has been characterized as the "dominant" paradigm, it warrants attention. After all, research techniques can be employed for evaluation purposes. Three basic research paradigms are the randomized control group, the matched comparison group, and self-comparison.

1. Randomized control group design necessitates random assignment of students to a treatment group (participants in a learning center activity) and to a control group (nonparticipants). This design provides the best assurance of any of the research approaches that the outcomes (student achievements and retention) were the direct result of participation in learning center activities. Random assignment is the best guarantee that students are initially equal on a variety of characteristics, including the skill in question or other indicators of academic potential. If, for example, there are fifty students who are interested in taking a study skills class, twenty-five will be randomly assigned to the class. Comparisons will be made between the two groups of academic success as indicated by GPAs and retention rates. Depending upon the criteria and the size of the sample, it is sometimes advisable to pretest the students.

This design poses several problems for assessment of a learning center problem. The major difficulty is random assignment of students to a control or no service condition. This stipulation is easy to meet in a laboratory experiment, but it is often impractical and sometimes unethical in the natural setting with human subjects. Some circumstances, however, can make it possible to meet the random assignment requirement. One such circumstance would arise if twice as many students apply for a course, program, or service as can be handled. If there is no rational system for making the service available, random selection of those who will be provided the service may be in order; the remainder will serve as the control group. Another possibility lies in delaying the service, if this can be done without harm. Under these conditions, one group gets the service first, while those on the waiting list group provide the control during that period. The status of the treatment or service group is compared to the status of the group on the waiting list, whose members have yet to receive the service. In the latter instance, it would serve to strengthen confidence in the conclusions to determine the status of the waiting list group after its members have received the service. If the service is having an effect, the waiting list group should make the same progress as the first treatment group.

However, it is likely that random denial of services to students — or waiting lists for services — run counter to the philosophy of the learning center. Thus, while this design has many merits, it will often be impractical. Campbell and Stanley (1966) elaborate on related design options.

2. In matched groups design, students who utilize learning center services are compared to students who do not, but no effort is made

to randomly assign students to a treatment or control condition. Instead, an attempt is made to compare students who use the learning center to students who are initially comparable on key characteristics, such as GPA and scholastic aptitude. Thus, if students who use the services are in the lowest quarter on scholastic aptitude measures and on academic probation, they will be compared to students showing similar characteristics. This design has relatively few practical problems, aside from the need for obtaining post measures from nonusers. However, it does have one major weakness, which imperils the inference that use of learning center services was the causal factor for positive outcomes, since it can be argued that those who select to use the services may be initially different from nonusers in motivation or in other ways, even if they are similar in aptitude. It may also be difficult to obtain truly matched groups of students. For example, if all students on probation are required to take a study skills course, there are no students left to serve as a match on this characteristic.

Statistical analysis can be used to patch up this design. One procedure is called covariance. While this procedure is no substitute for randomization, it can be used to adjust the posttest comparisons on the basis of the initial status of the two groups. In some ways, it is analogous to a handicap in golf or bowling in that the final achievement of the two groups is compared after they have been statistically equalized on the basis of their past records. The procedure is not perfect, but comparison is possible.

Another statistical procedure is to compare gain scores of the learning center group and the comparison group. If the learning center students increased their GPA by .5 of a grade point and raised their reading comprehension scores by 50 points, the meaning of these gains becomes clearer when compared to the gains of a group of students who did not use the services. However, the reliability of gain or difference scores is not high, so there is less confidence in the outcomes.

These approaches are often referred to as quasi-experimental designs. They differ from true experimental designs in that they lack the randomly selected control group. For an excellent discussion of the philosophical and technical issues, see Cook and Campbell, 1979.

However, it may not be possible to compare student users to any group but themselves. If *self-comparison* is the only resort, a premeasure is needed in order to establish a baseline to which their status at the end of the program or course can be compared. The pre-measure may be supplied by their GPA prior to using the service or by retention rates prior to establishment of the center. For such enabling skills as reading comprehension, it is necessary to pre- and posttest the students with a reading test.

Though this type of evidence is not as strong for causal explanations as that obtained with a random sample control group study, the weight of the evidence can be convincing. Evidence that a certain percentage have been removed from academic probation or completed an academic program may be sufficient, if it is dramatic enough or statistically significant. Besides working with group data, it is also possible to use single-subject designs to obtain and present information on changes in individual students (Kratochwill, 1978).

None of these three models are perfect if the criteria include practicality. An excellent research design is not necessarily a usable design. The evaluator and the learning center director should be aware of the trade-offs and make a choice based on the purpose of the evaluation and the intended audience. Both should guard diligently against compromising the philosophy and intent of learning center activities for the sole purpose of a cleaner research design.

DESCRIPTIVE MODELS. Almost every evaluation results in a report that describes the program and provides useful information. However, style and timing determine whether the report will fulfill this purpose (Newman, Brown, and Littman, 1979). Many evaluations result in reports which only by the greatest stretch of the imagination can be said to provide the reader with any idea of what the program was like. Too many provide information after the decisions have been made. Two approaches that avoid these problems are task analysis or systems models and case study approaches.

Task analysis models (Provus, 1971; Stufflebeam and others, 1971) provide analytic descriptions of program components as the program operates. These approaches are essentially systems models (Brown, 1979), which are outcome-oriented but still can be used in formative and process evaluation because they are concerned with outcomes at different stages of the program rather than solely with the final product. The focus is on determining the critical decisions and providing timely information. Program objectives are broken down into specific subgoals and arranged in a hierarchial order. At each decision point, what was expected is compared with what actually occurred. Criteria and standards are established, so that a decision can be made to revise the program component or to move on to the next. The resulting flowchart provides a description of the program in motion and makes it possible to revise the program when necessary. Task analysis approaches are generally quite helpful in formative evaluation.

Applied to a learning center, the case study approach can focus on one student, several students, or a group of students; more likely, however, it will be focused on one or two students. Instead of collecting a little information about a large number of students, a good deal of information will be collected about a few students. The activities and progress of one or several users of the learning center are described, and events related to their use of the center and subsequent accomplishments are documented in portrayal form. This approach and the resulting portrayal enables an audience to understand center activities through vicarious participation rather than tables, graphs, and statistics (Guba, 1978; Stake, 1976).

It is unlikely that a case study approach can stand alone as the evaluation of a learning center on a large campus, especially if the audience is external. Many will ask how typical the student portrayed is and what happened to other students. The case study approach can be very effective, however, when it is used to supplement other evaluation information. It can be used in conjunction with any of the evaluation strategies described in this chapter.

ISSUE-RESOLVING MODELS. Differing stands on issues exist between the external supporters and nonsupporters, between external persons and learning center staff, and even among individual learning center staff members. If the purpose of evaluation is to respond to these issues, the evaluation should be focused on them. This is particularly important if decisions will be based on these issues. Two closely related evaluation models are primarily concerned with issue resolution—responsive evaluation and transactional evaluation.

The emphasis of responsive evaluation (Stake, 1975) is on program issues and program activities. This is in contrast to many other models, which concentrate almost exclusively on program outcomes. The responsive evaluator determines the key issues, the information that relates to these issues, and the perspectives that different persons have on the issues and information needs. The evaluator visits extensively and regularly with staff, administrators, students, and others to share perspectives, validate interpretations, and determine whether the issues have changed. Unlike models that lay out a detailed evaluation and data collection design at the outset, the activities of the responsive evaluator are determined by the needs of the moment. Stake (1975) characterizes the responsive model as emergent and the others as preordinate. Outcome information is not necessarily excluded, but the emphasis is on issue recognition and program description.

The transactional model (Rippey, 1973) places even more emphasis on conflict resolution. It emphasizes early identification of the program's proponents and antagonists and determination of the kind of evidence that will be convincing to both. This model recognizes that many programs fail because of the covert as well as the overt hostility of administrators who feel that their powers are being usurped, of staff who have to change role expectations, and of others who feel threatened by the new program. These feelings and the resultant less than enthusiastic support are as likely to cause a program to fail as any other reason. Some suggest that the evaluator should be judged on the basis of the program's success (Walberg, 1973). It is the responsibility of the evaluator to see that conflicts are resolved and that energies are centered on improving the program. The emphasis is not on proving that the program is better than another program but on trying to make the program the best one possible. The transactional evaluator identifies with the program staff and the success of the program, even if he or she is external to the program.

Both approaches rely on evaluators who have good interpersonal skills, who can assist people in working through disagreements, and who understand and can work in a politically and emotionally charged environment. The evaluator must be in constant touch with the program and make frequent informal reports either along with or instead of a formal final report.

How Should Results Be Reported? How evaluation information is reported should be influenced by the nature of the audience and its information needs. The style of the report is probably most effective if it is conguent with the purpose of the evaluation and the nature of the information (Thompson, Brown, and Fergason, 1979). In many instances, there will be multiple audiences and, therefore, multiple reports (Brown, 1978). One useful form that the report can take is one or two pages written in a language and style that are readily accessible to a busy administrator or a lay audience. Highly technical reports are also essential, but they should be structured to provide information related directly to evaluation issues, questions, and potential administrative decisions.

Unique reporting strategies warrant attention when appropriate. These unique strategies include judicial hearings (Wolf, 1975) and the use of photography (Brown, Peterson, and Sanstead, in press). These reporting strategies also influence the evaluation activities, so a decision to use them should be made prior to the evaluation.

Conclusion

Believability and practicality are two major criteria for making political decisions. It is no coincidence that these criteria, usually described as credibility and utility, are also major criteria for a good evaluation. As in politics, trade-offs and compromises are inevitable. An external, formal summative evaluation will generally rate high on credibility but not necessarily on utility. An informal, internal formative evaluation may be highly useful but have relatively little credibility for an external audience. The types of evaluation and the strategies described are not necessarily mutually exclusive; in fact, they are often complementary. It is important to recognize that there is no one right evaluation scheme. The choice and decisions should be determined by the purpose of the evaluation.

References

Brown, R. D. "How Evaluation Can Make a Difference." In G. Hanson (Ed.), *New Directions for Student Services: Evaluating Program Effectiveness,* no. 1. San Francisco: Jossey-Bass, 1978.

Brown, R. D. "Key Issues in Evaluating Student Affairs Programs." In G. D. Kuh (Ed.), *Evaluation in Student Affairs.* Cincinnati: American College Personnel Association, 1979.

Brown, R. D., Peterson, C. H., and Sanstead, M. "Photographic Evaluation in Student Affairs." *Journal of College Student Personnel,* in press.

Campbell, D. T., and Stanley, K. J. *Experimental and Quasi-Experimental Designs for Research.* Chicago: Rand McNally, 1966.

Cook, T., and Campbell, D. T. *Quasi-Experimentation.* Chicago: Rand McNally, 1979.

Guba, E. G. *Toward a Methodology of Naturalistic Inquiry in Educational Evaluation.* Los Angeles: Center for the Study of Evaluation, University of California, 1978.

Kerlinger, F. N. *Foundations of Behavioral Research.* (2nd ed.) New York: Holt, Rinehart and Winston, 1973.

Kratochwill, T. R. *Single Subject Research.* New York: Academic Press, 1978.

Lenning, O. T., and McAleenan, A. C. "Needs Assessment in Student Affairs." In G. D. Kuh (Ed.), *Evaluation in Student Affairs.* Cincinnati: American College Personnel Association, 1979.

Lenning, O. T. (Ed.), *New Directions for Higher Education: Improving Educational Outcomes,* no. 16. San Francisco: Jossey-Bass, 1976.

McEwen, M. J. "Help for Pennsylvania's Culturally and Economically Deprived College Students." *Phi Delta Kappan,* 1979, *61* (4), 286-287.

Maxwell, M. *Improving Student Learning Skills: A Comprehensive Guide to Successful Practices and Programs for Increasing the Performance of Underprepared Students.* San Francisco: Jossey-Bass, 1979.

Newman, D., Brown, R. D., and Littman, M. "Evaluator Report and Audience Characteristics Which Influence the Impact of Evaluation Reports: Does Who Says What to Whom Make a Difference?" *CEDAR Quarterly,* 1979, *12,* 14-18.

Patton, M. Q. *Utilization-Focused Evaluation.* San Francisco: Jossey-Bass, 1978.

Provus, R. M. *Discrepancy Evaluation.* Berkeley, Calif.: McCutchan, 1971.

Rippey, R. M. (Ed.). *Studies in Transactional Evaluation.* Berkeley, Calif.: McCutchan, 1973.

Scriven, M. "The Methodology of Evaluation." In R. E. Stake (Ed.), *Curriculum Evaluation.* American Educational Research Association Monograph Series on Evaluation, No. 1. Chicago: Rand McNally, 1967.

Stake, R. E. *Evaluating the Arts in Education: A Responsive Approach.* Columbus, Ohio: Merrill, 1975.

Stake, R. E. *Evaluating Educational Programmes: The Need and Response.* Paris: Organization for Economic Cooperation and Development, 1976.

Stufflebeam, D. L., and others. *Educational Evaluation and Decision Making.* Itasca, Ill.: Peacock, 1971.

Sullivan, L. L. *A Guide to Higher Education Learning Centers in the United States and Canada.* Portsmouth, N.H.: Entelek, 1978.

Thompson, P., Brown, R. D., and Fergason, J. *The Impact of Evaluation Report Styles on Evaluation Audiences.* San Francisco: American Educational Research Association, April 1979.

Walberg, H. "Transactional Evaluation." In R. Rippey (Ed.), *Studies in Transactional Evaluation.* Berkeley, Calif.: McCutchan, 1973.

Wolf, R. L. "Trial by Jury: A New Evaluation Method." *Phi Delta Kappan,* 1975, *57,* 85-87.

Worthen, B. R., and Sanders, J. R. (Eds.). *Educational Evaluation: Theory and Practice.* Worthington, Ohio: Jones, 1973.

Robert R. Brown is professor of educational psychology and measurement at the University of Nebraska, Lincoln, where he has served as director of counseling and assistant vice-president for academic affairs.

*Contrasted to the traditional view of learning centers is one
that sees broad and integrative roles involving the
entire campus community.*

The Past, Present, and Future for Learning Centers

Oscar T. Lenning
Robbie L. Nayman

No one can deny that learning centers have flourished during the past decade, at least in terms of numbers. However, the view of the learning center on a typical college campus still tends to be very limited in its scope. We believe that, through creative effort, learning centers can become vital to a campus in many ways and that learning centers can assume forms and functions that even we cannot foresee. The authors of the preceding chapters in this sourcebook point to a number of expanded roles that can become viable for learning centers in the future. First, we will review those potential developments. Then, we will project what may be an even more imaginative concept for future learning centers.

A Review

As outlined in the opening chapter by Enright and Kerstiens, the concept of the learning center has greatly expanded since the first learning centers were developed to help military veterans improve their study skills during World War II. Even in the 1970s, however, as the number of operating learning centers approached 2,000, most learning

94

centers have been developmental or remedial in nature, and they continue to be viewed as efforts to apply new instructional technology that are separate from the main mission of the institution. Although Enright and Kerstiens point to a number of new services focusing on the entire student body that learning centers could provide and although some centers already provide such services, faculty and others on campus still see learning centers as developmental or remedial devices.

As Shaw points out, it is probably to the good at this point that faculty view learning centers as remedial and supplemental, because this makes them less threatening. As he states, "If the teaching is not remedial, then everyone can agree that it belongs in the college and university, that it should be done by regular faculty, and that traditional modes of teaching will suffice." As a member of a traditional university faculty who also administers faculty programs, Shaw is in a good position to know. However, as one who has become committed to learning centers and to the expansion of their roles, Shaw proposes a carefully tuned, participative strategy of long-term negotiation and discussion with faculty evolving from an initial focus on credit to eventual relationships of trust and respect. If this strategy is carefully followed, he believes, there is potential for learning centers to become integral partners and supporters of faculty even in such areas as student needs diagnosis, the facilitation of student cognitive development, the testing of experimental teaching and learning approaches, and faculty development.

Dempsey and Tomlinson speak to somewhat the same issue, but from the viewpoint of years spent developing and gaining faculty support for learning centers in a number of different campus settings. Starting with a focus on individualization of instruction and instructional and curricular improvements within the learning center and formal evaluations of progress therein, they show that there is potential for contributing to campus-wide instructional and curricular improvement. Like Shaw, they indicate that becoming involved in such campus-wide improvement is largely a long-term political process requiring the development of close and ongoing relationships with regular faculty.

Beal provides empirical evidence that learning centers can play major roles in improving student retention—probably the hottest topic these days, as postsecondary institutions seek ways to survive and remain vital as the traditional pool of prospective students continues to decrease. He shows that expanding the focus of learning centers to all students on campus and to a wide variety of activities holds the most promise for improving student retention, especially if faculty, administrators, and student affairs personnel all became involved and integrated into the effort.

As Dempsey and Tomlinson suggest, evaluation is important for further expansion of learning centers and for gaining campus-wide support. As Brown points out, the economic and political environment is such that learning center staffs will be increasingly called on "to provide evidence of worth and show whether they can do more for less." However, learning center staffs have largely ignored evaluation until very recently. Thus, the practical and feasible guidelines for conducting effective, improvement-oriented evaluations of learning centers provided by Brown should prove invaluable to learning center directors and staff who actively assimilate and apply those guidelines.

A Projection

The ideas that learning centers can serve all types of students in a variety of ways, research and test new teaching methods, and become intimately involved in assisting campus-wide curriculum and faculty development have already been discussed. The intention here is not to go beyond such purposes — we agree with such expansion of purpose — but to propose some additional ways in which the learning center concept could be expanded to achieve such purposes more effectively. Some writers believe that restructuring the form of the learning center and introducing staff with new types of skills, as well as reorienting and training current staff, could significantly improve the probability, effectiveness, and speed with which such new purposes could begin to be achieved. Even with structural changes, however, we are talking about a long-term and ongoing evolution. Such purposes cannot begin to be met overnight. Further, the costs and benefits of such changes will have to be re-evaluated periodically.

Let us begin with the concept of a learning center. The traditional concept is that the learning center is located in a single place on campus — for example, in the college library. The term *center* does not have to refer to location, however, and in the case of learning centers we believe that it should not. A learning center not only designates a service but reflects a philosophy — that of mobilizing campus resources to assist students and faculty to make maximum use of the learning environment. Hence, on many campuses it may be desirable for various functions of the learning center to take place at a variety of times and places. Some might even occur off campus, at student or faculty retreats, for example. Staff could be assigned to a variety of units — the library, the residence hall, the development center, the counseling center, faculty departments, the academic dean's office, the media center, or the student union. It may also involve getting faculty and students to interact more frequently and in modes that enable both faculty and students to feel comfortable, such as in living-learning centers or in programs that encourage faculty to invite students to their homes for informal activity.

The learning center could very well be conceived of as a system of centers, events, and activities with concurrent and complementary functions. Some functions, such as peer tutoring, could involve largely students; other functions, such as a faculty dorm visitation program, would largely involve faculty, and these activities could be either formal or informal in nature and actually coordinated by the center or merely encouraged to happen. Thus, a learning center may be other than a staff or set of staffs; that is, it may be a system involving communication and coordination among an array of functions and largely unrelated staffs and individuals across the campus.

To coordinate this wide diversity of functions and people, directors of the learning centers of the future will require much ingenuity, creativity, and skill in developing relationships and dealing with people at all levels. They will have to be specialists in the areas of gaining top-level administrative support and using incentives of all kinds. An example from the past that might be illustrative of what will be needed in the future was observed by one of the authors in the early 1970s. As coordinator of a consortium for follow-up evaluation at nontraditional colleges and universities, involving eight nontraditional and experimental colleges across the country, he was visiting the Office for Educational Development at the University of Wisconsin in Green Bay when he noticed some faculty members critiquing videotapes of one another's teaching. He asked how faculty could be motivated to become involved in such activity and learned that the chancellor had made a policy change requiring faculty to show concrete evidence of attempts to improve their teaching in order to be considered for promotion and tenure. The choice of evidence was their own, but it had been mentioned that the office for educational development was available to anyone who desired assistance, and that office suddenly had many faculty coming for help in this area. If the staff of this office had only told faculty that they would like to help, it seems likely that few would have taken advantage of that opportunity. Now, however, because of incentives that had been introduced by top-level administrators, faculty were taking the initiative and seeking out staff of the educational development office.

In addition to becoming an expert in the area of incentives and student, faculty, and staff relations, the director of a learning center in the future will need other skills and special involvement. For example, in response to the demand for lifelong learning and to the resurgence of emphasis on the teaching process in postsecondary education, a variety of opportunities and options for learning will become available to the general public for continuing education. Learning centers of the future will serve as brokers, as well as sources, of services. Champaigne (1980) discusses directions of learning centers in the year 2001 and notes that such centers will "act as intermediaries in connecting people who have requested a specific educational goal with people who can assist in meeting that goal—that is, public schools, industry, other higher educational institutions, informal learning groups, the military establishment, or proprietary groups. As providers, [learning assistance centers] would assist the student with formulation of educational plans or contracts; help to assess the learner's competency and style; provide the appropriate instructional vehicles; and assist in the evaluation of outcomes of instruction. To varying degrees, parts of this scenario have been and are happening" (p. 3).

Resurgent emphasis on the teaching process and individualization of instruction at the postsecondary level can provide opportunities for increased collaboration between faculty and learning center staff of the future in several ways. First, the design of new assessment, instructional, and evaluation modalities and the design of new modalities best suited to student needs and abilities will require specialized expertise that learning center staff can provide to the academic community. Second, the learning center of the future can play a pivotal role in institutional renewal by assisting faculty in developing and refining instructional skills, course design, evaluation, and media usage and by providing administrators and staff with opportunities for skill building through modularized and self-paced materials in specialized areas of knowledge. Third, because of the specialized skills of its staff, the learning center of the future can take the lead in producing a body of empirical and applied research on cognitive development and learning processes over the whole life span of the individual that should help to illuminate the changing character of learners in postsecondary education. Further, the basic tenet of college learning services—that they help students to "learn how to learn"—may well be broadened to include helping institutions to articulate the diverse cognitive skills and competencies that their curriculums require.

Finally, learning center staff of the future will increasingly become involved in what Banning (1980) terms management of the campus ecology. The current and projected influx of new students to postsecondary education and their enormous heterogeneity in terms of ethnicity, gender, social class, abilities, skill deficits, and expectations will necessitate increased attention to the identification and amelioration of student/environment mismatches. Adoption of an ecological perspective, which focuses on the interactive processes between student characteristics and all dimensions of the campus environment—people, curriculum, policies, campus traditions, values, and attitudes, services, and physical facilities — will sensitize learning center staff to environmental factors that can enhance or impede student progress and prompt collaboration with faculty and staff to designing of a more growth-producing campus environment.

Thus, special involvement in campus affairs for the learning center staff of the future will be wide-ranging and encompass such varied activities as participating in the interviewing of and advising on all new faculty and staff candidates, assisting with orientation of new faculty and staff, development and inservice training to current faculty and student affairs staff, and consulting with academic deans and other campus policy makers to interpret learning and developmental needs of new student constituencies.

Through an expanded range of concerns, learning center staff of the future can participate in setting an ongoing, total-campus tone regarding student learning and its facilitation. Undoubtedly, skills and involvement that we cannot even begin to imagine in 1980 will become important in the future.

Resources for Further Reading

A growing body of literature is focused on the learning center as a concept. An excellent synthesis of this literature is contained in the book by Maxwell (1979). Martin and others (1977) offer a manual for development of postsecondary learning centers with particular emphasis on the conceptualization and administration of such centers. Peterson (1975) discusses the learning center from the perspective of a four-part model that comprises a multimedia library, audiovisual services, nontraditional learning spaces, and instructional development. For a survey of the status of learning centers in the late nineteen seventies, see the report by Sullivan (1978). Beal and Noel (1980) provide a good picture of the role that learning centers are playing in student retention. Lenning, Beal, and Sauer (1980) present a thorough review of research and theory, which points out significant factors and interactions that are underpinnings of student retention, and provide a theoretical and empirical base from which evidence and a defensible rationale for expanding learning centers to new areas can be drawn to gain support for such change. A similar theoretical and empirical base with respect to student development is provided by Baird (1976), Schalock (1976), Moore (1976), and Terenzini and Pascarella (1979, 1980). For a more general assessment of the efficacy of basic skills programs, reports by the Committee on Learning Skills Centers (1976) and Grant and Hoeber (1978) are informative.

References

Baird, L. L. "Structuring the Environment to Improve Outcomes." In O. T. Lenning (Ed.), *New Directions for Higher Education: Improving Educational Outcomes,* no. 16. San Francisco: Jossey-Bass, 1976.

Banning, J. H. "Management of the Campus Ecology." In U. Delworth and G. Hanson (Eds.), *A Handbook for Student Services.* San Francisco: Jossey-Bass, 1980.

Beal, P. E., and Noel, L. *What Works in Student Retention?* Iowa City, Iowa: American College Testing Program, 1980.

Champaigne, J. R. "2001: Future Directions of Learning Assistance Centers." Paper presented at annual convention of the American College Personal Association, Boston, April 1980.

Committee on Learning Skills Centers. *Learning Skills Centers: A CCCC Report.* Washington, D.C.: National Institute of Education, 1976.

Grant, M. K., and Hoeber, D. R. *Basic Skills Programs: Are They Working?* Research Report No. 1. Washington, D.C.: American Association of Higher Education, 1978.

Lenning, O. T., Beal, P. E., and Sauer, K. *Retention and Attrition: Evidence for Action and Research.* Boulder, Colo.: National Center for Higher Education Management Systems, 1980.

Martin, D. C., and others. *The Learning Center: A Comprehensive Model for Colleges and Universities.* Grand Rapids, Mich.: Central Trade Plant, 1977.

Maxwell, M. *Improving Student Learning Skills: A Comprehensive Guide to Successful Practices and Programs for Increasing the Performance of Underprepared Students.* San Francisco: Jossey-Bass, 1979.

Moore, W., Jr. "Increasing Learning Among Developmental Education Students." In O. T. Lenning (Ed.), *New Directions for Higher Education: Improving Educational Outcomes,* no. 16. San Francisco: Jossey-Bass, 1976.

Peterson, G. T. *The Learning Center—A Sphere for Nontraditional Approaches to Education.* Hamden, Conn.: Shoe String Press, 1975.

Schalock, H. D. "Structuring Process to Improve Student Outcomes." In O. T. Lenning (Ed.), *New Directions for Higher Education: Improving Educational Outcomes,* no. 16. San Francisco: Jossey-Bass, 1976.

Sullivan, L. L. *A Guide to Higher Education Learning Centers in the United States and Canada.* Portsmouth, N.H.: Entelek, 1978.

Terenzini, P. T., and Pascarella, E. T. "Student-Faculty Contacts and Freshman Year Educational Outcomes: A Replication." Paper presented at annual forum of the Association for Institutional Research, San Diego, May 1979.

Terenzini, P. T., and Pascarella, E. T. "The Influence of a Living-Learning Experience on Selected Freshman Year Educational Outcomes." Paper presented at annual forum of the Association for Institutional Research, Atlanta, April 1980.

*Oscar T. Lenning, senior associate at the National Center for
Higher Education Management Systems (NCHEMS),
joined the NCHEMS staff in 1974 after eight years on the
research staff of the American College Testing Program.*

Robbie L. Nayman, senior psychologist, University Counseling Center and assistant professor, Department of Education, Colorado State University, is past chairperson of Commission XVI—Learning Centers in Higher Educaton, of the American College Personnel Association (ACPA).

Index

A

Access, complications of, 7
Accountability, to students, 52
American College Testing Program (ACT), 60, 62
Andrews, G. A., 2, 3, 18
Angus, S., 6, 18
Anxiety reduction, 46–47
Astin, A. W., 59, 73
Attrition. *See* Retention
Auburn University, tutoring at, 69

B

Baird, L. L., 98, 99
Balanoff, N., 8, 18
Baldwin Wallace College, credit course at, 71
Bamman, H. A., 6, 18
Banning, J. H., 97, 99
Beal, P. E., vii, 59–73, 94, 98, 99
Bear, R. B., 3, 4, 5, 18
Behrens, H. D., 2, 3, 18
Bergman, I. B., 10, 18
Blake, W. S., Jr., 6, 7, 18
Bloom, B., 7
Bock, J. D., 9, 18
Bond, J. A., 4, 18
Book, W. F., 2, 3, 18
Brabham, R. D., 23
Brooks, M., 14, 18
Brown, E. T., 8, 19
Brown, R. D., vii, 75–92, 95
Brown, S., 10, 19
Brudner, H., 15, 19
Buchanan, P. C., 42, 57

C

California: access in, 2; community college peer tutoring in, 7
California, University of, Berkeley, computer-assisted course at, 49
California, University of, Irvine: adjunct classes at, 44; credit classes at, 51–52; flexible grouping at, 49
California, University of, Riverside, adjunct classes at, 44
California State University, Dominguez Hills, adjunct classes at, 44
Campbell, D. T., 86, 87, 91
Carman, R. A., 1, 9, 19
Carpenter, T., 10, 19
Champaigne, J. R., 97, 99
Charters, W. W., 3, 4, 19
Christ, F. L., 1, 8, 9, 15, 19
Clark, R. E., 11, 14, 19
Clymer, C., 1, 16, 19, 23
Cognitive-style mapping, 14
Columbia University, and entrance requirements, 2
Committee on Learning Skills Centers, 98, 99
Communication arts, 5–6
Computer-assisted instruction (CAI), 8, 17, 49–50
Computer-managed instruction (CMI), 8, 17
Cook, T., 87, 91
Cope, R. G., 59, 73
Cowgill, S., 21
Crafts, G., 15, 19
Credit: dangers of, 32–33; developmental view of, 31–32; and instructional/ curricular change, 46, 51–52; issue of, for faculty, 13, 29–33; pragmatic view of, 30–31
Creedon, C. F., 60, 73
Cross, K. P., 7, 10, 11, 13, 14, 19, 48, 57

D

De Anza College, computers used at, 49, 50
Dellans, M., 46, 57
Delong, G. H., 5, 19
Delta Community College, flexible scheduling at, 51
Dempsey, J., vii, 41–58, 94, 95
Deterline, W. S., 7, 19
Devirian, M. C., 9, 19, 23
Donisi, P., 8, 19
Drob, H. A., 1, 22
Drummond, R. J., 14, 19
Durkee, F. M., 7, 20

E

Eckert, R. E., 2, 3, 20
Ellison, J., 1, 8, 9, 20
Enright, G., vii, 1–24, 44, 57, 93–94
Evaluation: case study approach to, 88–89; cause and effect models of, 85–88; criteria for, 83–85; defined, 76–78; descriptive models for, 88–89; establishment phase of, 78–81; external and formal versus internal and informal, 77, 81, 83; of faculty change, 85; formative versus summative, 77, 81, 83; impact assessment phase of, 83–90; installation and improvement phase of, 81–83; of institutional change, 85; issue-resolving models for, 89–90; of learning centers, 75–92; models for, 85–90; program versus personnel, 77–78; reporting on, 90; research versus, 76–77, 85–86; responsive, 89; scheme for, 78–90; of student change, 84–85; task analysis models for, 88; transactional, 89–90

F

Faculty: and academic competency, 25–39; attitude of, 11, 25–26; and credit, 13, 29–33; evaluation of change among, 85; future roles for, 36–39; and instructional/curricular change, 51, 53–54; involvement of, 35–36; negotiating with, 33–35
Faculty development, learning center role in, 4, 16, 38–39, 54, 97
Fergason, J., 90, 91
Field dependence/independence, 14
Fleming, D. R., 14, 23
Florida, University of, reading program at, 4, 6
Fraley, L. W., 10, 20
Fusario, J. F., 8, 20

G

Garland, M., 2, 10, 20
G.I. Bill, 5
Gibson, A. D., 15, 19
Grand Valley State Colleges, tutoring at, 69–70
Grant, M. K., 98, 99
Green, T., 44, 58
Greenbaum, B., 11, 20

Gregory, J. W., 6, 7, 20
Guba, E. G., 89, 91
Gulf Coast Community College, credit courses at, 71
Gunselman, M., 1, 20
Guskin, A. E., 11, 20

H

Hagstrom, J., 13, 20, 48, 57
Handleman, C., 13, 20
Hannah, W., 59, 73
Harvard University, and entrance requirements, 2
Havelock, R. G., 54–55, 57
Henderson, D. D., 10, 20
Hertz, S. M., 13, 20
Hoeber, D. R., 98, 99
House, E., 53, 56, 57
Houston, University of, verbalization process at, 43
Hultgren, D. D., 10, 20
Husson College, noncredit sessions at, 71–72

I

Indiana, University of, failure rate at, 2
Instruction: collaboration to improve, 53–56; and evaluation, 53; flexible format and curriculum for, 50–52; flexible time and place for, 50–51, reform of, 41–58
Instruction, individualized: in affective factors, 45–47; flexible and self-instructional, 48–50; modules for, 47–48; in skills development, 45

J

James, B., 50, 57
Jencks, C., 15, 20
Johnson, A., 10, 20
Jones, E. S., 2, 3, 20
Jones, R. C., 8, 21
Jones, Y., 10, 19

K

Kazmierski, P. R., 10, 21
Kemp, J. E., 5, 15, 21
Kendrick, S. A., 8, 21
Kerlinger, F. N., 76, 91
Kerstiens, G., vii, 1–24, 93–94

Kirk, B. A., 8, 14, 21
Knoell, M., 7, 21
Kratochwill, T. R., 88, 91

L

Lamar University: credit courses at, 70-71; tutoring at, 68-69
Lane Community College, Study Skills Center at, 8
Learning: in adjunct classes, 43-44; to learn, 2, 44, 97; process, 42-44; by verbalization of process, 42-43
Learning centers: and able students, 51; and abstraction, 34; accountability to students by, 52; administrative responsibility for, 4, 6, 8; affective cognitive approaches in, 13-14; assistance versus resources in, 10-11; and campus ecology, 97-98; as change agents, 41-42, 54-56; components of, 9; concept of, 1-2, 9, 95-96; and credit, 13, 29-33; credit courses at, 70-71; delimited, 9; from 1850 to 1940, 2-3; establishment of, and evaluation, 78-81; expanded role for, 1-24; and faculty, 25-39; feasibility of, 80; in fifties, 5-7; in forties, 3-5; full-range programs by, 66-68; future of, 16-17, 95-98; history of, 1-10; impact assessment for, 83-90; individual attention in, 44-50; individual components evaluated in, 82-83; installation and improvement of, and evaluation, 81-83; institutionalization of, 17; and instructional/curricular reform, 17, 41-58; intended services of, 82; issues current in, 10-16; and learning-disabled students, 11-12; and mastery learning, 13; materials for, 4; need for, 26-27; needs analysis for, 78-80; noncredit courses at, 71-72; number of, 9, 75; and process learning, 42-44; and program improvement, 82; programmed materials for, 6, 7-8; publications and associations for, 16; and receptivity, 80-81; resources on, 98; responsibility for, 27-29; review of, 93-95; in seventies, 9-10; in sixties, 7-8; status and stature of, 15-16; student opinions on, 83; supportive services by, 37-38, 64; target population for, 11, 63-64; as threat to faculty, 27-28; tutoring at, 68-70; users of, 81-82

Learning disabilities, defined, 12
Lenning, O. T., vii-viii, 59, 63, 73, 78, 85, 91, 93-100
Lewis, J. A., 48, 57
Lippitt, R., 42, 57
Littman, M., 88, 91
Locus of control, 14
Lombardi, J., 12, 13, 21
Longview Community College, tutoring at, 69
Loop College, full-range program at, 66
Luskin, B. J., 8, 24

M

McAleenan, A. C., 78, 91
McAllister, J. M., 12, 21
McCarthy, M. M., 12, 21
McClung, C., 11, 15, 21
McEwen, M. M., 78, 91
McGann, M., 3, 4, 21
Macken, E., 8, 23
McPherson, E., 1, 2, 9, 11, 13, 15, 21
Maguire, L. M., 42, 57
Maloney, J., 49, 57
Malpractice, 12, 32
Marquette University, reading and study skills programs at, 6-7
Martin, D. C., 98, 99
Martin, R. G., 14, 21
Mathews, T., 15, 21
Maxwell, M., 1-2, 3, 5, 6, 7, 8, 10, 14, 15, 21, 48, 57, 75, 80, 91, 98, 99
Mayfield, C. K., 10, 16, 21
Mayhew, L. B., 56, 57
Meierhenry, W. C., 7, 21
Melloni, B. J., 10, 20
Merren, J., 9, 22
Merrill, I. R., 1, 22
Metropolitan State College, adjunct classes at, 44
Middleton, L., 59, 73
Mink, O. G., 9, 14, 22
Minnesota, University of, reading program at, 4
Minnesota, University of, Morris, tutoring at, 70
Missouri, University of, Kansas City, full-range program at, 67-68
Moore, W. Jr., 15, 22, 98, 99
Morgan, W. E., 2, 22
Morningstar, M., 8, 23
Mount Mary College, tutoring at, 68

N

National Center for Higher Education Management Systems (NCHEMS), 60, 62
National Training Laboratories, 42, 57
Nayman, R. L., vii-viii, 93-100
Neidt, C. O., 8, 22
New York University, reading laboratory at, 3
Newman, D., 88, 91
Newman, L., 7, 22
Noel, L., 59, 61, 73, 98, 99
Northern Iowa, University of, full-range program at, 66

O

Objectives, and learning center development, 6-7
Ohio State University, reading program at, 3
Ohlone College, minicourses at, 49
Oregon, University of, credit classes at, 52

P

Pan American University, full-range program at, 67
Pantages, T. J., 60, 73
Park, Y., 1, 22
Parr, F. W., 3, 22
Pascarella, E. T., 98, 99
Patton, M. Q., 77, 91
Peterson, C. H., 90, 91
Peterson, E., 10, 20
Peterson, G. T., 2, 9, 13, 16, 22, 98, 99
Pflug, R. J., 12, 22
Piaget, J., 44
Pierce Junior College, full-range program at, 67
Pinette, C. A., 19
Pitman, J. C., 7, 22
Pittsburgh, University of, credit course at, 71
Pressey, L. C., 3
Princeton University, and entrance requirements, 2
Provus, R. M., 83, 88, 91

R

Raygor, A. L., 7, 22
Reger, R., 12, 22

Rehabilitation Act of 1973, Section 504 of, 12
Remedial, as term, 5, 28-29
Remedial programs, failure of, 8
Research: evaluation versus, 76-77, 85-86; matched groups design of, 86-87; randomized control group design of, 86; self-comparison design for, 87-88
Retention: learning center role in, 9-10, 59-73, 79; programs for, 63-72; research findings on, 61-64; study of, 60-61
Richlin, M., 6, 23
Riesman, D., 15, 20
Rippey, R. M., 89, 91
Robinson, F. P., 2, 3, 4, 22
Roueche, J. E., 2, 7, 8, 9, 11, 13, 14, 15, 22, 46, 57

S

Saettler, P., 5, 10, 22
San Bernardino Valley College, Learning Center at, 8
San Diego City College, adjunct classes at, 44
San Jose State University, minicourses at, 49
Sanders, J. R., 76, 91
Sanstead, M., 90, 91
Sauer, K., 63, 73, 98, 99
Schalock, H. D., 98, 99
Scriven, M., 77, 91
See, S. G., 9, 22
Self-concept, 14
Sharp, S. L., 2, 3, 4, 22
Shaughnessy, M. P., 7, 23
Shaw, J. W., vii, 25-39, 94
Sherman, J. F., 10, 20
Simpson, R. G., 4, 5, 23
Skinner, B. F., 6, 7
Smith, G. D., 9, 19, 23
Smith, K. G., 16, 23
Smith, R. K., 19
Snow, J. J., 2, 8, 11, 13, 15, 22, 46, 57
Spache, G. D., 3, 6, 7, 23
Spann, N. C., 9, 15, 23
Spaulding, N., 49, 57
Spivey, N. N., 14, 23
Staff: and evaluation, 77-78, 80-81, 82, 83; issues of, 14-15; skills needed by, 96-97
Stake, R. E., 89, 91

Stanley, K. J., 86, 91

Stephenson, J. V., 21

Students: able, and learning centers, 51; accountability to, 52; evaluation of, 52; evaluation of change among, 84–85; learning-disabled, 11–12; opinions of, 83

Stufflebeam, D. L., 88, 91

Sullivan, L. L., 1, 9, 23, 75, 91, 98, 99

Sullivan, R. J., 12, 23

Summers, E. G., 7, 22

Suppes, P., 8, 23

Swindling, J. A., 10, 23

T

Tappan, H. P., 2

Terenzini, P. T., 98, 99

Thomas, C. L., 8, 21

Thompson, P., 90, 91

Tobias, S., 46

Tomlinson, B., vii, 10, 23, 41–58, 94, 95

Tomlinson, M. D., 10, 23, 44, 58

Touhey, J. F., 9, 23

Touton, F. C., 2, 23

Towson State University, noncredit sessions at, 72

Tresselt, M. E., 6, 23

Triggs, F. O., 3, 4, 23

U

Utica College, noncredit courses at, 72

V

Vargas, E. A., 10, 20

Von KleinSmid, R. B., 2, 23

W

Walberg, H., 81, 90, 91

Walker, C., 11, 23

Walker, G. H., Jr., 3-4, 5, 24

Watson, J., 57

Watson, N. E., 8, 24

Weaver State College, tutoring at, 69

Weber, C. B., 6, 24

Weiner, N., 5

West Liberty State College, full-range program at, 68

Westley, B., 57

Whimbey, A., 42–43, 58

Whipple, G. M., 2, 24

Whittier College, full-range program at, 67

Williams, G., 8, 24

Williams, R., 14, 24

Wisconsin, University of, Green Bay, faculty development at, 96

Wittenborn, J. R., 3, 5, 24

Witty, P. A., 3, 5, 24

Wolf, R. L., 90, 91

Woolley, J., 7, 24

Worthen, B. R., 76, 91

Y

Yale University, and entrance requirements, 2

Z

Zerga, J. E., 3, 24

New Directions Quarterly Sourcebooks

New Directions for College Learning Assistance is one of several distinct series of quarterly sourcebooks published by Jossey-Bass. The sourcebooks in each series are designed to serve both as *convenient compendiums* of the latest knowledge and practical experience on their topics and as *long-life reference tools*.

One-year, four-sourcebook subscriptions for each series cost $18 for individuals (when paid by personal check) and $30 for institutions, libraries, and agencies. Single copies of earlier sourcebooks are available at $6.95 each *prepaid* (or $7.95 each when *billed*).

A complete listing is given below of current and past sourcebooks in the *New Directions for College Learning Assistance* series. The titles and editors-in-chief of the other series are also listed. To subscribe, or to receive further information, write: New Directions Subscriptions, Jossey-Bass Inc., Publishers, 433 California Street, San Francisco, California 94104.

New Directions for College Learning Assistance
Kurt V. Lauridsen, Editor-in-Chief
1980–1981:   1. *Examining the Scope of Learning Centers*,
                Kurt V. Lauridsen

New Directions for Child Development
William Damon, Editor-in-Chief

New Directions for Community Colleges
Arthur M. Cohen, Editor-in-Chief
Florence B. Brawer, Associate Editor

New Directions for Continuing Education
Alan B. Knox, Editor-in-Chief

New Directions for Exceptional Children
James J. Gallagher, Editor-in-Chief

New Directions for Experiential Learning
Pamela J. Tate, Editor-in-Chief
Morris T. Keeton, Consulting Editor

New Directions for Higher Education
JB Lon Hefferlin, Editor-in-Chief

New Directions for Institutional Advancement
A. Westley Rowland, Editor-in-Chief